The
CHILD IN CRISIS

The
CHILD IN CRISIS

Patricia Doyle and
David Behrens

McGraw-Hill Book Company

New York   St. Louis   San Francisco   Bogotá   Hamburg
Madrid   Mexico   Milan   Montreal   Panama
Paris   São Paulo   Tokyo   Toronto

The young people described in these chapters are real. Some identifying facts have been altered to respect confidentiality.

First McGraw-Hill paperback edition, 1989

1 2 3 4 5 6 7 8 9 FGR FGR 8 9 2 1 0 9 8

ISBN 0-07-004366-3

LIBRARY OF CONGRESS CATALOGING-IN-PUBLICATION DATA

Doyle, Patricia.
  The child in crisis.
  Includes index.
  1. Problem children—United States—Case studies.
2. Emotional problems of children—Case studies.
3. Depression in children—Case studies.   4. Parenting.
I. Behrens, David.
HQ773.D68   1986   649'.154   85-23886
ISBN 0-07-004366-3

*To my parents, Harrison and Ruth, and my
children, Kellee and Lee and Kevin, for helping me
to understand this difficult task of parenting. And to
Leo, who has helped me to see it all more clearly.*

P.D.

*For Mildred and Mary Lou, mothers who walked the
parental path with courage.*

*For Randy, the little boy whose pain
set this work into motion;*

and for Tyler, who contributed his skills.

D.B.

CONTENTS

INTRODUCTION

The Chinese character for the word "crisis" is made up of two parts. One is a symbol for danger. The other is the symbol for opportunity.

The nightmares of adulthood come early for thousands of youngsters, a notion that often stuns the parents of young children and adolescents.

Depression and attempted suicide at age five?

Psychosomatic illness at six?

Unexplained "accidents" at nine?

Drinking and drug problems at thirteen?

Sexual acting-out at fifteen?

For many parents, the problems are staggering, impossible to understand or accept. The idea of children troubled with depression and anxiety seems alien, the dark side of premature adulthood. The gardens of youth are recalled often as having more roses than thorns. Parents may rhapsodize childhood—and the melodies linger on: "Just a kid again . . . Doin' what I did again . . . Singin' a song . . . "

But many children, from preschoolers to teenagers in late adolescence, are in trouble today. For millions of families, a child in crisis is a fact of daily life. Our portraits are drawn from the lives of real people: the young and the very young. We will seek the roots of their troubles and suggest how parents can spot the early warning signs and help their children. We will also suggest ways of parenting that might prevent many problems from reaching the crisis stage.

Some of the stories may seem familiar. Others may be startling:

Randy, the five-year-old who did not want to live.

Jane, who refused to eat—and grow up.

Sharon, who seemed to lose her hearing at age eight.

Jim, who wondered if his car accidents were deliberate.

Dana, who had her first abortion at fifteen.

Sid, a lonely teenager who found a friend in drugs.

Some of these young people were assisted by therapy and counseling. Others were aided by adults who recognized their needs in time. But in almost all cases, early intervention by parents, teachers, or other caring adults might have eased their pain.

The stories of these children show that the stuff of crisis is ordinary enough—loss of a friend, death or departure of a parent, fear of a new neighborhood, worry about school, the breakup of a family.

Dana, for instance, was drawn to a young man who was distant, like her father. Sid's world was shaken when his parents broke up. Sharon lost her hearing after her grandfather moved to another city. All of them had to deal with painful feelings of abandonment. But in most cases, other factors also came into play. Often explanations and solutions are elusive, complex.

Childhood depression is a controversial subject. Can children, like adults, suffer from clinical depression—anger turned inward? The question is still being debated. But formal definitions aside, health care workers in community clinics claim that they are seeing a steady increase in cases of depression among young people, even the very young. It is clear that many childhood miseries are—and always have been—a dramatic potpourri of suffering. They include:

Learning problems.

Underachieving.

Mysterious ailments.

Obsession with food.

Acting-out in school.

Misconduct at home.

Running away.

Drug and alcohol abuse.

Sexual experimentation.

Unwanted pregnancy.

And as a final resort, suicide.

Trickle-Down Misery

Many of these problems—especially suicide—were once perceived as the exclusive province of adults and older adolescents. Now they seem to be seeping down to the very young. Suicide among the young has been well documented for almost twenty years. In the decade of the 1970s, for instance, the number of young children who committed suicide in the United States averaged 155 a year. All were between ages five and fourteen. The total reached 167 in 1981, according to the National Center for Health Statistics.

The unknown is even more frightening: No one knows how many other children, teens and pre-teens, have suffered or are now suffering from unrecognized depression. How many have tried to commit suicide, one way or another, without success or recognition? How many have ended their lives with acts of violence that were classified as accidents?

Some were children who were hit by cars, who fell down a flight of stairs, who tumbled out of a window, who cut themselves accidentally, who strangled themselves while "playing" with a rope, or who suffered some other mishap—recorded as an accident in official police records, incorrectly or deliberately, in some cases to save parents additional grief or embarrassment.

Why So Young?

Once sadness in childhood might have seemed like a contradiction in terms. Why does it seem so commonplace now? Our social scientists have rounded up the usual suspects: Divorce on the rise . . . the increased number of working mothers . . . more single-parent homes . . . the influence of television as surrogate parents . . . economic hardships for millions of families . . . the lack of feeling special in a community . . . the breakdown of public schools as a support system and a source of discipline.

All these factors may play a role. But then, why can some children weather the storms of social change while others tumble into psychic turmoil? The larger questions remain.

On these pages, we will suggest that some of the answers can be found by looking at particular lives—at the everyday events that shape children's lives but may go unnoticed by busy parents coping with their own problems. The crises of childhood take many forms: Some children starve themselves; others overeat. Some have nightmares; others are insomniacs. Some drive cars recklessly, experiment with drugs, or get pregnant. Others wet their beds, deny the onset of their sexuality, and hold on to their childhood.

The danger signals can be subtle—an unaccountable loss of appetite or stomach aches, forgetfulness or fearfulness or fatigue. Children may bring home unexpected reports of misconduct from school. Their fights with brothers and sisters may escalate at home. With adolescents, sexual adventures may be a danger signal. But not always.

It is also difficult to determine what should evoke a smile and what should sound the alarm. What kind of behavior is normal, and what kind reflects deep-rooted depression or anxiety? Is disobedience a warning sign or just part of growing up?

To some extent, parents must expect disagreeable behavior, rebellion, and antagonism. But how much? What kind? Some can be normal and natural throughout childhood and adolescence. Can parents tell when their child is truly in crisis?

In these pages, we stress how crucial parental awareness is—knowing what is happening at school, knowing what is happening at home and what has happened in the past that might be shaping the present. When a child acts out, is it in a way that demands attention? If a teenager gets drunk at a party, does he or she stagger home noisily, making sure the entire household is aware of the event? Listen carefully for messages behind the masks.

Sometimes the answers can be linked to old traumas, such as a divorce, a death in the family, or other loss. Sometimes a recent separation can stir jolting emotions from the past. A child may enter a new school or neighborhood and suffer old feelings of abandonment and anger—feelings that are rooted in early childhood, such as the birth of a new brother or sister.

What really counts is your being there. Be aware of the events that touch the lives of your children most deeply. Keep an eye open for the events that set off feelings of abandonment and anger. They do set the groundwork for crisis, sometimes subtle, sometimes blatant. And most of all, keep the dialogue going.

Meeting Randy

In the following pages, we will examine many crises of childhood and we will see how mothers and fathers can respond. Of all crises, the most frightening—and perhaps most mystifying—is a child's impulse to end life.

It was true in Randy's case, until his parents stepped in and began to explore why a five-year-old felt so sad. For his parents, it was hard to accept: a child who did not want to live. But as those who meet and work with children testify, the very young sometimes carry the heaviest burdens. We begin with Randy's story.

The
CHILD IN CRISIS

WANTING TO DIE

Randy: A close call

Three months before his sixth birthday, Randy tried to kill himself.

It was a cloudless day, an ordinary day in June without a hint of disaster or desperation. In the cool of mid-morning, Randy's mother, Rita, was buying groceries at the local market. She liked the old neighborhood, frayed but friendly, where everyone looked out for each other.

Just before noon, after chatting at the checkout counter, Rita headed home. It was getting hot. In the stillness of the late morning, she could feel the sidewalks baking.

Balancing two shopping bags, she walked slowly past the rickety houses with patches of earth beside the front steps. It was a good working-class neighborhood, filled with children, like the one she had grown up in.

A half-block from her corner, she glanced across the backyard fences. She could see her own house. Oh, it was really too small, she thought. She and her husband, Larry, had lived there for eight years. But now they had a teenaged daughter and three young sons. The house needs painting too, she reminded herself. It was a bit of a daydream. Then her reverie ended. Something snapped.

Her eyes caught an image she did not expect. It seemed to travel in slow motion to her brain. When it completed the journey, it took her breath away. She felt a rush of adrenalin and her heart pounded. Was it terror? No. It was more like a dream.

A little boy, wearing brown shoes and no socks and a pair of short gray pants, was hanging out of the bedroom window on the top floor. His thin body dangled half in and half out, legs limp, his body balanced on his belly on the window sill. He just hung there, about 25 feet above the concrete patio, where the family held backyard cookouts on hot summer nights. From a distance, there was a momentary mirage effect: It looked like a two-dimensional photograph of a small child pasted onto the back wall of an old house.

It was not a picture. It was her son, suspended between life and death. At first she couldn't be sure if it was Bobby, her nine-year-old, or Randy. Both had the same blue pajamas. Then she screamed: "RANDY!"

Shopping bags locked in her hands, Randy's mother ran full speed around the corner and down the block, still screaming. Her husband Larry, who worked nights, was sitting in the small dining room. When he heard his wife's screams, he raced up the stairs. Randy was still there, hanging out the attic window, a bit dazed, distracted, deciding.

Larry pulled him in. Randy didn't resist. He seemed more indifferent than afraid. When Larry carried Randy downstairs to the kitchen, Rita reached out to hug him but he jerked away. He was like ice. At first, he didn't respond at all.

"Why did you do that?" she asked Randy. "You could have been hurt, you could have been killed."

Randy just stood there, glum.

"Why?" his father asked him.

Randy finally answered. "I don't like it here," he said. "I hate it. I hate this house. I hate it here."

He spoke in a monotone, staring ahead like a zombie, as if nothing had happened. Rita thought about the time when Randy was an infant. He was always such an affectionate baby.

What had happened? Why did he climb out of the window like that?

"You could have died," his mother said again.

"I wanted to die," Randy said.

The Road to Disaster

Randy's story is a chilling one: The notion that a five-year-old child might want to die is almost too staggering to grasp. For most adults, the idea is alien, freakish, a contradiction in terms. Childhood is supposed to be filled with joys and hopes and tender loving care. Isn't it?

Not necessarily.

The deaths of well over 100 young children have been recorded each year for the past fifteen years. All of them were aged five to fourteen, all were suicides. As always, the unknown is even more frightening: Randy's suicide attempt on the morning of June 9, 1980, would not have turned up as an official statistic. If he had died, his leap to death on a backyard patio would probably have been recorded as an accident, just another sad ending to a foolish prank. At the time, Randy's parents, Rita and Larry, were not even aware their son was moving along a disaster course, a path as involuted as a detective story.

On the evening of June 8, 1980, the night before he tried to kill himself, Randy wore his shoes to bed. Under his blue pajamas, he wore his play clothes. He always did that. Was something wrong? His parents sensed there was, but then, they were preoccupied with the problems of their other children. And wasn't Randy just going through a "difficult" age? He did mope. He refused to play with other children. And often, he locked himself in the bathroom. His parents would hear voices: Randy's invented playmates.

There were other troubles, too. Randy's grandmother had just died. And after months of clashes with her parents, Randy's sister, Kathy, had moved out of the house and into her aunt's home. His sister and his parents had often argued about her curfew hours and coming home late and hanging out with older boys. When the yelling began, Randy fled. "He'd run up to his room and be gone," Larry said.

Randy's brothers had their own troubles. Bobby, the oldest boy, was having learning problems in school. Donny, the youngest, was suffering from asthma and had recently been hospitalized. "So all our attention went to the other kids," Rita said. And Randy was left alone. He had never been the kind of child who asked for attention. "He always seemed so contented," his mother said. But his kindergarten teacher was worried. There, Randy withdrew, refused to answer questions or play with other children. He would sit alone, stony-faced.

And at home, he was aloof, unaffectionate. "If I tried to hold him, he'd pull away," his mother said. "And I guess I must have pushed him away without realizing it. I'd get annoyed with him when he'd ask questions or show me a toy. I'd say: 'Not now, Randy, please!'"

The pattern became clear only after the suicide attempt, although in retrospect, Randy's parents felt that they should have seen it: Randy was so moody. He was so fearful of conflict. He played alone. He went to bed early, sometimes right after dinner. He squirreled away all his possessions, even unimportant objects.

"He'd keep everything, even little papers he'd pick up on the street," his mother recalled. He'd put them in a little bag and take it to bed with him. They were his things. He'd be very upset if one of his brothers touched them."

Going to sleep was a ritual. "He'd take a bath and get into his pajamas," his mother said. Then he'd take his pajamas off, put his clothes back on, and pull his pajamas on over his clothing.

Randy was lucky. His parents were baffled, but they cared and, most of all, they knew how to ask for help. After the near-disaster of June 9, Randy's mother asked a friend, who had just returned to college, for advice. Her friend, in turn, spoke with a school psychologist, who suggested a visit to a children's clinic at a local hospital. Rita had never heard of the clinic, even though she lived only a few minutes away. "It was a miracle, because we had no idea where to turn."

So on June 27, 1980, Randy began once-a-week sessions with a psychiatrist at the clinic. Treatment began slowly and demanded patience. In the early weeks, there was silence and petulance: The door to Randy's anger was locked. But soon, phantoms emerged:

The "Neck-Chopper Man" and the "Mother Killer" were among them.

So some of the secrets of Randy's pain began to unravel. Over the next eight months, Rita and Larry lived through difficult days. But it was also a period of discovery.

Since Randy showed no signs of committing other self-destructive acts, he was treated as an out-patient. Randy and his mother came to the clinic once a week, and both of his parents came in regularly for family counseling sessions. Randy was withdrawn, easily fatigued, given to severe temper tantrums, unable to play with other children. It was a portrait of a little boy in crisis.

In the beginning, Randy said little—except that he hated his family and wanted to die. Failing to function at home or in school and unable to handle the stresses in his young life, Randy was moody, alone, and excessively angry with his parents and other people who cared for him.

Later, when Randy felt better, he exhibited even more anger. It was a healthy sign, but it had its dark side too. In such cases of acute depression, the recovery period can be dangerous, since a child such as Randy might feel more energetic—may try to kill himself again.

A Door Opens

At first, Randy sat close to his mother's side in silence. "It took at least four sessions before Randy got out of his chair or even looked at the doctor," his mother said.

Then there was a breakthrough. "The doctor told Randy he could play with any of the toys in the office, and he found a dollhouse he liked. It had dolls for all the family members—father, mother, brothers and sisters."

With the dolls, Randy invented two families. "The doctor asked Randy if he wanted to name the doll-people and he did," his mother said. "He gave them our names. I was the mother of one of the families, and my daughter Kathy was the mother of the other family. The children in each family had the same names—Randy, Donny, and Bobby—and Larry was the father in both families."

Randy began to play with the dollhouse every week, moving the doll figures in and out of the house. One afternoon, he pretended that one of the houses was on fire. "He put his Randy doll into a toy fire engine and started off to rescue the other dolls," his mother recalled. "But instead of saving them, he started running down the other doll-people with the fire engine. He ran them down over and over again. He did this a lot in the next few weeks and it was always violent. It would start off nicely and always end up violent, with him killing all the people in the family. It was frightening." And his most deliberate target was the mother-doll.

Rita avoided scolding her son. She'd never say, "Oh, that's terrible," or "Don't do that." She was advised to hear Randy out, to allow him to express anger without interfering. So she would say something like, "Oh gee, you're pretty angry at them, aren't you?" when Randy showed his rage.

Randy always referred to the doll as "the mother," not "my mother" in these sessions. But it was safe to assume that Randy's anger was directed at his own mother.

Sometimes, Rita would sit on the floor and join the doll game. "At first I'd try to move the doll-people out of the way, but Randy would come right after them with the fire engine. I just watched and didn't scold him." The process allowed Rita to become the mother both she and Randy wanted her to be—without the therapist becoming a surrogate mother. Rita became a regular part of play therapy, and in the late summer, Randy and his mother began to work with Play-Doh, the popular modeling clay.

Randy liked to make monsters, his mother said. Big monsters and little monsters. Monsters with two heads and four arms. He seemed to enjoy being the creator, being in control of the scary things he was shaping. His mother would play, too. She would make happy animals—camels with humps, elephants with trunks, big-shouldered bears. They all had wide smiles on their faces.

Randy ignored them at first, preoccupied with his own world of nightmarish figures. Then, one day, he went over to the play table, hunting for something. Finally he found it: a ruler with a sharp edge. Sitting down on the floor again, he began to chop off the heads of all the smiling animals his mother had made.

When he was asked who was attacking the animals, Randy said: "The Neck-Chopper Man."

It was the first time Randy's mother had heard the phrase, and it scared her. Her first reaction was shock. Inside, she felt like screaming, "For God's sake, don't talk that way." But she remained silent. Was the Neck-Chopper Man very angry? Randy was asked.

"Yes," the little boy replied.

The Neck-Chopper Man was not only angry, Randy said. He was also very powerful and important. He really scared the animals because he was so big and strong. He could do whatever he liked. Sometimes he'd let the animals escape with their lives, and sometimes he'd kill them. And with the emergence of the Neck-Chopper Man, the heads of many Play-Doh animals rolled during the following weeks.

Who was the Neck-Chopper Man?

The Neck-Chopper Man was a perfect personification of Randy's aggressions. Here were these animals, created by his mother, and Randy could threaten them. He may not have been aware how angry he really was, but it was good to make the animals feel as weak and sad as he felt—a normal childhood fantasy, which may frighten some parents if they do not understand why it is happening.

Play therapy provided Randy with a way to express his anger and then to put his anger into words. When he felt he was permitted to be angry, his anger surfaced and its nature became more clear.

By the end of the summer, Randy seemed to be responding to therapy and special attention. Even as his play grew more angry, he seemed more relaxed and more independent of his mother.

Then there was an accident. On September 6, 1980, the family celebrated Randy's sixth birthday. It was a Saturday afternoon, and all the neighbors were invited to a backyard party. "Randy was doing so well, we decided to have a big barbecue," his father said.

Midway through the party, before the birthday cake was served, the celebration ended. Randy's cake had been placed on a table in the center of the patio. There was also a large urn, filled with boiling coffee. Randy was eager to see the inscription on the cake and leaned on the edge of the table. The urn of boiling coffee tipped over.

Instinctively, one of the neighbors pushed Randy back so the coffee would not burn his face. Scalding hot, it spilled across his chest and stomach. Larry remembered chasing after his son.

"He spun away and ran down the driveway, screaming. I grabbed him and we dumped him into the little pool in the yard next door." His skin was peeling off his chest and he yelled: "Daddy, please don't let me die."

The Turning Point

Looking back on Randy's year of crises, his parents think that the summer accident was a turning point. Suffering from severe burns, Randy was taken to a burn center in New York. Randy remained in the hospital for ten days. Today, the burn scars are still there but the trauma may have had a positive side. "When he was up in his room, thinking about jumping out the window, he probably knew he could stop it," his mother said. "But this accident—it was as if he really was afraid of dying for the first time."

Perhaps it was the first time Randy sensed that death was permanent, that it meant "not coming back again." The accident at the party might have been an unconscious self-destructive act, but it is difficult to support that kind of speculation. In any case, Randy thrived.

In the hospital he received much extra attention, which was beneficial because he had felt so deprived. His family rallied around him and, for the first time, Randy really felt he was important to them. When Randy received letters from his therapist, he was so happy that he hung them up in his room.

At first he didn't talk about the accident, but he finally asked his mother how he had been burned. He remembered running up the alley, and he wondered how he could have run if he was so hurt. Later, Randy asked his father: "Daddy, why did God do this to me?"

Rita was relieved that Randy did not blame her. Since

treatment had begun, Randy had been much more affectionate. "He'd give me a hug and I'd hug him back. But after he burned himself, he withdrew again for a time. I thought he was angry at me since I was standing near him and I didn't stop it."

A few weeks after returning home in mid-September, as therapy resumed, Randy entered first grade. Since both his parents were spending more time with him, Randy was more cheerful. He seemed less hostile toward his mother, more cooperative at home, and more able to express his feelings. By early fall, Randy began to mix with his classmates and, for the first time, risked competing in games with his brothers.

Randy's parents played a creative role in their son's recovery. They were supportive from the start, even though they were having trouble themselves in communicating and expressing anger. In the family therapy sessions, they talked about new ways to function with their children.

At first, Randy's parents blamed each other for the chaos in their home. They were overwhelmed and depressed and resentful about their family life.

But slowly, they altered their own lives, each giving Randy more of their time. Larry recalled his feelings: "We were really acting like a family."

A machinist, Larry had worked nights, often coming home after the children were off to school. "That summer, I made a big point of spending more time with the kids, and I started to take Randy places I never did before, like the store or the garage and ball games. Places I always took Bobby. And his mother and I would sit down and talk to Randy alone, for a half-hour or so. Like it was his special time. So he wouldn't feel left out."

They had discovered one of the roots of the problem: "I was spending time with Bobby and his mother was always worrying over Donny. Nobody was with Randy."

Larry's feelings toward Randy were also a factor. A shy man, Randy's father was far less comfortable with people than his oldest son, Bobby, who was a good athlete and made friends easily. It made Larry proud. But Randy reminded him too much of himself—withdrawn and introspective—and without wanting to, he grew more distant from Randy.

The departure of Randy's sister from the household was also traumatic. Kathy had served as a warm and comforting surrogate mother. When she left, he felt even more alone.

In therapy, Randy began to talk about his brothers and about school. He didn't like his brother Bobby, he said. Bobby was always doing things with his father. If Bobby was there, he was afraid to try things. Bobby always won in games. He hated Bobby.

About this time, Rita and Larry brought in Randy's two brothers for several sessions. Randy loved it. "For the first time, Randy was running everything. He'd tell them: 'Do this' and 'Don't do that' and 'Put that over there.' He was in his own domain." For Randy, it felt good, after feeling so vulnerable for so long.

In the fall, Randy talked more about school and showed off his first-grade work. But at times, he refused to dress himself for school. So Rita drew up a calendar and gave Randy stars for doing ordinary things, like dressing himself and going to school without arguing.

"If he put on his pajamas at night, I'd gave him a star. If he did his homework, I'd give him another star. Then, at the end of each week, he would receive a prize or a treat," his mother recalled.

The behavior modification approach worked. Randy was very proud of the stars and seemed to take pride in what he was doing. "We would paste the stars on the calendar in his bedroom, and he was very pleased," his mother said.

By now, Randy saw the world with greater clarity. In one session, his mother made a smiling clay lion. Accidentally, Randy knocked its head off.

"The Neck-Chopper Man is back," he said.

His mother said: "We haven't seen him for a long time."

"Oh, he's been away," Randy said.

The incident may have reflected Randy's struggle to work out his anger with his mother. Soon after, he was asked to draw a picture of his family. Everyone was the right size except Randy who was twice as big as his brother Bobby. "I guess that's how he wanted to feel," his mother said.

That autumn, Randy's willingness to take risks was even

more evident. Previously, he had been afraid to be second best to his brothers or other children. But now he was ready to challenge. His anger had been too frightening for him at first, but when he learned that he could express it without being squashed, he was no longer afraid to be more outgoing and aggressive.

Larry remembered a joyous fall night at an amusement park in the Rockaways. Randy and his brothers had been playing a horse-racing game, and for the first time, Randy won. He became very excited, jumping up and down. "I beat them . . . I beat my brothers . . . I can beat them," he shouted.

Randy hopped around and around, holding his hands high up in the air, Larry recalled. "It was like he'd just become champion of the world."

Coming Back

In January 1981, Randy shared a special moment with his mother. Rita was feeling very sad one day because a cousin had just lost a child. She mentioned her feelings and started to cry. She explained that she was sad because the baby had been special to its mother, just as Randy was very special to her. And Randy came over and gave her a big hug.

In mid-February, Randy was discharged from therapy. He missed the trips to the hospital, having his mother and the doctors all to himself. And he was glad he could visit the hospital whenever he wanted to. But Randy has never returned.

That spring, on a weekend afternoon, Rita and Larry sat at their dining room table, recounting the story of their family crisis. Randy raced in, breathlessly. He had been playing down the block.

He was a cute little boy with shaggy hair and ruddy cheeks and a smudgy face, a sort of urban Huck Finn. He was a New York Yankee fan, he said. "And the Kansas City Chiefs in football." He really liked the neighborhood boys' club where Randy and his father went three or four evenings a week, and he was doing well in the table-tennis and checkers and the basketball-shooting tournaments. He also liked hockey and touch football. Still breathless, he was off and running again—out the door.

Rita thinks her son's case is almost a miracle. Just after he turned 8, he entered third grade. Still very quiet in school, he had made new friends and, with them, he didn't seem so shy. In kindergarten, before therapy, Randy had seemed to have learning problems, but when he underwent a series of special tests later, his mother said, "he was so far ahead, his teacher was amazed."

The tests in second grade had showed Randy reading at a fourth-grade level and doing third-grade math—not bad for a little boy who had been so sad not so long ago.

No one can be certain if Randy fully understood what suicide meant at the time. Perhaps he was not able to connect the notion of death with "never coming back." But his mother is sure that Randy did really want to end his young life.

Soon after, Randy seemed like a different child. The suicide attempt and his experiences at the clinic did not come up in day-to-day conversations. His work at school continued to improve and his spirits were upbeat. Only one shadow from his early childhood seemed to recur.

"It happens when Randy hurts himself badly, like getting a really bad bump or scrape," his father said. "He'll run up to me and cry: 'Daddy, I don't wanna die. Please don't let me die.'"

Listening with Care

When children such as Randy suffer from severe depression, they are prime candidates for suicidal thinking. The warning signs of depression in younger children can vary and may include some or all of the following symptoms:

- Disturbance in sleeping patterns—with the child sleeping either too much or too little.

- Difficulty with concentration, at home and in school.

- Hyperactivity.

- Excessive sadness.

- Bizarre behavior, such as squirreling away objects as Randy had done.

- Withdrawal from family and friends.

Asking a child who demonstrates some of these symptoms why he or she is behaving in a bizarre or unfamiliar way—such as gathering all his possessions or saving bits of string and scraps of paper—does not produce answers, since the child is unlikely to know the reasons.

It might be more useful to explore the child's feelings in a simple way. For example:

"Are you feeling badly tonight?"

"Do you feel like talking?

"You look like you're about to cry. . . . Why do you feel so sad?

"You seem to have so much trouble paying attention when we talk. . . . Do you feel worried about something?

"Sometimes it seems like you've gone away and I miss you."

These statements and questions let the child know that parents are nearby, aware of them and willing to be with them, no matter how bad the child is feeling. It can also open up communication, since the child is invited to talk about whatever he or she is feeling.

Possible warning signs of adolescent depression and suicidal thoughts are somewhat similar. They may include:

- A change in eating and/or sleeping habits.

- A drop in grades at school.

- A loss of interest in favorite activities.

- The loss of a sense of humor.

- Withdrawal from friends, classmates, and family.

- Abuse of alcohol or other drugs.

- Sudden decisions to give away valued possessions.

- Talk of suicide.

Listening carefully to any talk about suicide is vital. It should be taken seriously, no matter how far-fetched it seems to parents or other adults. The point cannot be stressed strongly enough.

The events that precipitate feelings of deep depression and suicidal thinking also vary in both younger children and adolescents, and in some cases, they may seem less serious to the outside observer. But changes such as the loss of contact with a friend, a parent, or a sibling, such as Randy's feelings of loss when his sister moved away, can have great impact.

And there are many other feelings of loss experienced by children. An adolescent girl, discovering or fearing she is pregnant, may feel a sharp loss of status and self-esteem. A child who moves into a new neighborhood or into a new school can feel rejected and unwanted. When such feelings lead to talk of suicide, it is crucial that parents give the signals their full attention.

FAILING IN SCHOOL

For many children, failing in school is their first painful collision with the real world.

Leaving home for the first time, of course, is a momentous step—both frightening and intriguing. Once in the world of the classroom the excitement and illumination of learning can be a new adventure. But for some children there is only loneliness and pain—traumatic times that often can be avoided.

There are many reasons why school becomes an obstacle course for children. In the following pages—looking at the early lives of Cindy and Jim—some of the causes will emerge, throwing light on the ways in which parents may help their own children.

Cindy and Jim's experiences were a test for both their families. Cindy, whose sister did everything right, could not learn no matter how hard she tried. Jim, who was a bright young man, felt that he never could try hard enough.

While not all learning problems have an emotional basis, one pattern recurs: Failure in school brings lowered self-esteem.

The pattern was true for Jim and Cindy, and both, typically, were prompted to act out against themselves, an expression of anger and pain.

Often, children whose parents have high expectations for them can be overwhelmed by anxiety, and will be unable to concentrate. And these children may unwittingly use failure in school to punish their parents and themselves. But failure in

15

school is often related to complicated patterns within the family, as in the case of Cindy, who could not learn to read, and of Jim, who failed to live up to his parents' great expectations.

Cindy: Learning was hard

No one ever knew about the rope.

Cindy had found it near the clothesline in a backyard down the street. She kept it in a box of toys under her bed, and one afternoon, when she had been sent up to her room—punished again for a temper tantrum—she took out the rope and tried to hang herself.

Cindy was nine years old at the time. She did not talk about the suicidal episode for years. No one else knew about it, but Cindy recalled the incident clearly: Making a noose, like the ones in the cowboy movies. Slipping it around her neck. Throwing it over a hook on the back of her closet door. But then the hook broke. Somehow it didn't work the way it did on TV. Nothing she ever did turned out right.

Cindy does not remember what else happened that afternoon, but she still recalls her feelings. "I thought a lot about killing myself, about how bad my parents were going to feel. I really wanted them to feel as bad as I did at the time," she said years later in a therapy session.

Cindy had always felt angry at her mother and father, although at the time she did not know why. Perhaps it was having to go to school. She hated school. Nothing ever seemed to turn out right there, from the time she began first grade.

The teacher, for instance, would write homework assignments on the blackboard, and everyone would copy them. Everyone but Cindy. Somehow, she could never write all of it down. Then, after dinner at home, there would be big fights with her mother and father.

"Where is your homework assignment?"

"How come your sister never has trouble in school?"

"Why are you always so difficult?"

The words still ring in her ears. Cindy never could explain how hard she tried in school. Over the dinner table there would be harsh words and angry looks, and Cindy would be sent to her room. Often, she would stay there for hours, sulking.

Alice, her younger sister, was never punished. In fact, everyone loved Alice. But Cindy wasn't sure she loved Alice at all.

She remembered the accident in the car. Once, she slammed a car door on her sister's hand. Cindy was about seven years old at the time.

"My mother was driving me to a friend's house one afternoon, and Alice was in the car too. It was an icy day and when I got out and was shutting the door, I slipped. I didn't realize my sister had her hand on the top of the door. I pushed the door closed and it crushed her hand. Alice screamed in pain and my mother became hysterical. We all rushed to the hospital. Alice had a broken finger but my parents seemed so angry with me, as if I had killed her. As if I did it on purpose. My father said later, 'Why can't you be more careful with your little sister?' "

Just a few months earlier, she had been riding a training bike with little wheels in the back. Without meaning to, she ran into her sister. Alice wasn't hurt that time, but her mother blamed her for not being more careful. Cindy felt overwhelmed by guilt. Her parents were right, she felt: She could never do anything right. That's why they loved her sister more than they loved her.

One of Cindy's most painful experiences was the loss of her father's affection. Or so she remembered it. Until she was five or six years old, Cindy recalls, her father seemed so loving. That was before she started school. Cindy loved to sit on her father's lap and look at the pictures in the Sunday newspapers, or watch the football games on TV while her father dozed off in his easy chair.

Little by little, she felt shunted aside. Her younger sister received all the cuddling. Fathers don't hug and kiss big girls, she was told. Her mother had never been affectionate anyway, Cindy recalled. So now she felt there was no one at all to hug her. And across the room, there was Alice, sitting on her father's lap. She was sure her sister was better than she was.

Cindy's first three years in school were hellish. She was too bright to fail, but she was always frightened. She could not read. Writing was arduous. She was learning to hate school.

At home, Cindy's failures were always under intense scrutiny by her parents.

"What's the matter with you? Another D in spelling! What were you doing—dreaming?" her mother would ask.

Indeed, Cindy was day-dreaming. This is one of the things children do—an avenue of escape, when they are so frustrated that they don't understand their schoolwork and their teachers embarrass them in front of classmates.

Some talk to kids in the next row.

Some get up and walk around the room.

Some get headaches or hit other kids or run away.

Cindy day-dreamed all the time.

And she missed even more classwork. Her parents were frantic, more critical than ever. Her sister, after all, was having no trouble learning to read and write. But in a class of thirty-five youngsters, no one caught on to what really was happening to Cindy.

No one even speculated that something might be wrong with the educational process. Cindy's parents were both college educated, but they grew up with the attitude that the teacher was always right and good childen did well. That was simply a given.

By third grade, Cindy's self-esteem was sagging. School was a daily terror. She was unable to do anything right, beset by anxieties that would last a lifetime.

Then, just by chance, when Cindy was entering fourth grade, her Aunt Ruth, a teacher who was taking graduate courses, made a startling discovery—and it changed Cindy's life.

Her aunt, who had come from California on a visit, had been testing a new reading exercise on her niece. Just for fun. And she discovered that Cindy suffered from dyslexia—experiencing extensive letter and word reversals, such as seeing the word "dog" as "god," for instance. Cindy's aunt also discovered that her niece was a bright little girl despite her serious reading disability. And she played a crucial role in turning Cindy's life around.

Cindy was lucky.

Diagnostic textbooks stress that early detection and treatment is crucial in cases of dyslexia, before a pattern of frustration and failure is entrenched. Often, such feelings can lead to delinquency and other behavior problems, emotional withdrawal, and alienation from parents, teachers, and other children.

For Cindy, a new learning process began just in time. Her aunt had discovered that her niece was so bright that she had been able, to some degree, to compensate for her reading disability. Having trouble recognizing some words, she was able to cover up the problem by a complex system of shortcuts, by learning other things more quickly.

Teachers and parents had not detected her problem earlier, and the years of feeling inadequate had taken a heavy toll on Cindy's emotional life. By now, she was convinced that something was seriously wrong with her.

For years, in fact, Cindy continued to feel isolated and inadequate, although later she was successful in high school and went on to college and a career in textile design. Looking back as an adult, Cindy still remembers her aunt's discovery as a magical moment. Because of her aunt's imagination and insight, Cindy's teachers at school began a special program of individual after-school instruction, trying new teaching methods. And soon, Cindy began to read.

"That this wonderful woman should have come along," Cindy muses. "It opened a whole new world to me. After that, she always had a special place in my heart." When she recalls the memory, tears come to her eyes.

The Power of Parents

The discovery was crucial: Cindy was not stupid. Not a freak. But she still felt she was different. Much harm had been done in her early years. So while the process of learning in school accelerated, her self-esteem was badly damaged. It took years to rebuild, and even today the shadows of her learning problems haunt her.

At a professional conference, for instance, a speaker will outline a new and complex idea. Suddenly, Cindy will feel that she cannot follow the words and ideas of the speaker. Her heart will race and she will feel as confused as she did when she was in first grade, unable to follow the speaker's train of thought.

The old childhood anxieties will return, even though she is aware—consciously—that the subject matter is in fact difficult, that everyone around her may be having trouble understanding an unfamiliar subject. For a while though, Cindy will feel like a small child again.

Later, in therapy in her early twenties, Cindy recalled memories of other experiences that shaped her feelings of low self-esteem.

One Sunday afternoon, just after her eleventh birthday, she went to a neighborhood movie with her father. Cindy proudly carried a new, very adult purse—a birthday gift from her father. In the theater, she put the purse on the empty chair beside her. As they were leaving the moviehouse, she discovered that her purse had been taken by someone.

Cindy was devastated.

So bereft, so guilty, Cindy was unable to express her feelings of loss and hurt. To compound the wound, her father seemed irked. He did not have to say anything to make Cindy feel scolded. The disapproving look on his face said it all. Cindy remembers that she forced herself not to cry. But her father's anger made it even more impossible for her to explain how really sorry she felt.

"I never did tell him," she recalled.

If only she had been asked, she would have poured out her heart. But then, she had spent years repressing her most vulnerable feelings. So once again, she toughed it out with eleven-year-old petulance. Becoming sullen and withdrawn, hurting very much on the inside, feeling under attack again, she only mumbled: "It's not my fault." And that was that.

There were similar disappointments.

When she was in high school, Cindy once bought a second-hand phonograph from a schoolmate. She was very excited about the bargain. But then she discovered that the turntable didn't work properly. She was so relieved when her father wandered past her room. He was so smart. Perhaps he could fix it.

Instead, her father was annoyed and critical. How could Cindy have thrown away good money on such junk? How could she buy a machine that didn't even work?

At that crucial moment, Cindy's father was not aware of the enormous power he held—to hurt her or to make her happy. Devastated again, Cindy withdrew and said nothing. And perhaps her father felt it was just another case of his daughter expressing her defiance, her old moodiness once again. "To this day, when I think of my father's scoldings, it makes me feel like crying," Cindy said.

Unlocking Emotions

Many adults, confronted with challenging situations they do not understand, will often experience anxieties. Most adults, however, have learned to control them, to take another look at what they do not comprehend. They may ask questions or consult a book.

But children like Cindy, unsure of themselves, become overwhelmed by confusion and the recurring sensation that once again, they can do nothing right.

Why is that so frightening?

The process is simple enough. A teacher would ask Cindy to read and when she looked at the words, they would make no sense to her. But unlike children with greater self-esteem, she was unable even to formulate a question. Tongue-tied, she was too scared to ask for assistance. And often, her defensive reaction produced the most frightening effect: Her teacher would berate her.

Once again, she would be humiliated, the way she was at home when her parents compared her to her sister Alice, who did everything with such ease. No wonder it seemed as if her father loved Alice more than her. Her sister always played a crucial role in Cindy's inner life. Even as an adult, she still blames herself for Alice's childhood accidents.

Cindy was only five or six at the time but her sister was a potent rival. And when she was the victim of accidents, it was an unconscious wish come true for Cindy. Cindy still felt overwhelming guilt about those incidents.

At those times, Cindy had needed comforting, but her parents were too upset to recognize Cindy's needs. Perhaps they did not understand the unstated war between siblings, the surging feelings of jealousy and competition that brothers and sisters often harbor for each other.

It is helpful to avoid placing blame. Cindy, for instance, might have been encouraged to express her feelings of jealousy. Her parents might have noticed Cindy's forlorn look and observed:

"You look sad today."

If Cindy did not respond, a more specific approach might have worked.

"Sometimes when Alice sits on Dad's lap, you seem to feel unhappy."

Her mother might have added: "Sometimes when you feel badly, you might wish Alice was somewhere else."

It is another way of saying: "It's all right to feel badly, to have angry thoughts, even when you wish for a moment that your sister disappeared from the face of the earth."

Instead, Cindy felt guilty. Later, she acted out her guilt with a hapless attempt on her own life.

Bad Feelings, Good Messages

It is important to encourage children to express their emotions. Parents will often find the expression of emotion in younger children easier to accept. But as children grow older, they often are expected to contain the expression of feelings with which parents are uncomfortable.

The feeling most often discouraged by parents is anger—a natural and healthy emotion that, like all other feelings, needs to be expressed. When it is not expressed directly, it will either be turned inward and cause depression or it will be expressed in some other destructive way.

Anger that is expressed directly, in fact, need not be destructive, and its expression will enhance the relationship between parent and child. Parents can serve as role models for their children by verbalizing their own anger. For example, a parent may say: "I get so angry when you leave your bike in the driveway!"

They can also encourage and support their children's direct expressions of anger. If a child seems moody or withdrawn, a parent might say, "You seem upset. Would you like to talk about it?"

Sadness is another feeling that many parents discourage in their children, often without meaning to. But their children's sadness often will set off memories of their own sad moments when they were children. And many parents wish to avoid these feelings. If children never see their parents express sadness, they are likely to adopt the same style of expression and withhold emotions themselves.

Once again, if a child seems unusually quiet, a parent might ask: "Is everything all right? You seem sad today."

By keeping questions direct but neutral, parents still can be caring and available. They can show that they relate to their children's emotional life—by recognizing it, by accepting its reality, by empathizing with it.

It is a way of signaling many things:

- "It's okay to feel the way you do."

- "I'll take care of you while you're feeling badly."

- "I'm not here to criticize your feelings."

- "I'm not leaving you."

It is easy to forget the pain of childhood. As adults, some fathers and mothers may prefer not to resurrect the painful memories of their own growing-up. But to truly empathize, it is useful to remember those days—and perhaps to feel some of the pains again.

It is a trip back into childhood—to understand what their sons and daughters are feeling. It is possible to discover with relief: "Oh my God, that's what I once felt." And the expression of reassuring messages to your children may flow more easily. These messages Cindy never heard, and her own anger was more difficult to bear alone.

Jim: The underachiever

Jim was day-dreaming. On a Friday afternoon, driving home from school, he felt a strange impulse: to crash into a tree. The urge drifted across his mind, like a shapeless shadow, he recalled later. Just for an instant, he felt impelled to swing the automobile's steering wheel sharply to the right and collide with something. There was no conscious reason for the feeling—and then it was gone.

Thirty minutes later, Jim did crash. Swerving to avoid a slowing car, he collided with an old station wagon parked along the side of the country road.

Jim was not hurt. Just scared. But he vividly remembered his feelings a half-hour before the accident. And when he told his mother about the incident, she insisted that Jim seek psychological counseling. It was the third car accident he had had that year.

"You must see someone," she said.

Jim followed his mother's directive and discovered later that his accidents on the road may have served as a set of warning signals from the deepest recesses of his being.

Good Is Not Good Enough

Jim was seventeen and a junior in a good private school. He came from a comfortable middle-income family. His father was an middle-management executive with a large electronics firm, and his mother worked part-time, teaching a course in English literature twice a week at a community college. His sister, Georgia, born when Jim was two years old, was earning good grades in junior high school, much better than Jim had done.

Georgia's school work pleased Jim's parents because both of them believed in "achievement" and in the obligation of making a "contribution" to their community. To their friends, they were a portrait of a successful and confident couple, with a devotion to intellectual success and two bright children who shared their values.

Jim was a popular young man, but he had been feeling uneasy about himself for the past two or three years, at least since he was fifteen. Always self-critical, he berated himself for not doing better in school. In fact, his lack of achievement prompted his parents to enroll Jim in a private school. Jim's acceptance by a good college had always been a high priority.

Often, Jim procrastinated over school work, unable to finish term papers and other school projects. On exams, time always seemed to run out. Music was another litmus test for Jim. Like his father, he was an accomplished pianist. Yet he found no satisfaction in music, feeling his progress was too slow.

Later, Jim recalled early clashes with his father over his music lessons. He had been nine or ten years old and very excited about his new-found talent. Every evening, after dinner, he would practice for an hour in the family's small music room off the dining room.

But the practice sessions soon became an ordeal. From the living room, his father would call in, commenting on his mistakes, criticizing his work. Jim felt humiliated. After all, his father was so good at everything he did. And even though Jim was practicing in another room, he felt his father was standing right there, looking over his shoulder. By age 11, he took flight, practicing in school instead, convincing a music teacher to permit him to use the piano after classes had ended. Nothing he did, he felt, ever would make his father happy. But when he was a little boy, he never was able to put these feelings into words.

Jim's father had also studied piano when he was a child, and had gone on to major in music during his early college years. But he did not pursue a career in music. It would have been too risky, too difficult to earn a decent income for his future family, he decided. Instead, he went into a business

25

management program and settled into a comfortable but dead-ended executive position with a large and paternal corporation.

At age forty-five, Jim's father was not a happy man. He felt he never had fulfilled his own potential. Perhaps he should have accepted more daring challenges as a young man, following his impulse to study music. An underachiever himself—a man who had never forgiven himself for his own unattained dreams—he was disappointed when Jim, his surrogate, failed to succeed for him.

Early Failure

Jim began to have problems in second grade. While he learned to read, his school marks were just average. It was surprising to teachers, since he scored above average on IQ tests. In class, however, he was just able to keep up to minimum standards, failing to excel as his parents had expected.

"We know he's bright, but often he doesn't seem to pay attention," one of his grade school teachers told Jim's father.

Another teacher reported: "He seems to drift off."

Jim did manage to keep up. He had no behavior problems . . . did not cut class . . . avoided drugs and the drinking crowd. But there was something wrong. Only with the support of occasional tutors and his parents did Jim complete ninth grade with a middle-of-the-class average.

Then his parents decided that Jim ought to attend a prep school, where he would receive special attention. Jim was happy about the change, glad to attend a new school and to live on the campus, returning home only on weekends. Although he presented a placid exterior, he had been unable to avoid dinner-time clashes with his father. During his grade school and junior high years, the dining room table had become a battlefield, and for Jim, prep school was an escape hatch.

As Jim grew older, his father seemed to become more and more critical. He would berate his son's mediocre marks and his low test scores. The conflicts were frequent but modulated, always low-keyed. In Jim's family, no emotion was ever fully expressed. Confronted by his father's anger, Jim would snap back with caution. But his response made his father even more angry, and Jim would scurry back into silence.

Inside, Jim felt devastated by criticism. When he did answer back, he felt cut in two by his father's responses. And after each fight over the dinner table, he felt even more worthless.

The messages from his father were always double-edged. Jim recalled, for example, the time he had failed to complete a long term paper for a ninth-grade English class. His father was furious.

"You never finish anything you start," he said, his voice filled with anger. Then, more calmly, he added, "You know, Jim, it's only that we care about you so much that we want you to do well, for your own good. We know you can do better."

By now, Jim believed that indeed something was wrong with him. His parents certainly did care about his welfare, but nothing ever worked out right. Why didn't anyone understand that he just couldn't concentrate? Jim felt depressed all the time.

In private school, despite the smaller classes, Jim drifted along with mediocre grades. And he was lonely. Often, he changed roommates, unable to find anyone he really felt comfortable with. No one seemed to have just the right combination of traits he wanted in a friend or roommate. They were either too neat but dull or too smart but messy. He was unable to accept anyone for what they were. They had to be perfect. Just the way he was supposed to be. Finding perfection was a lonely job.

Later, in therapy, Jim began to learn a good deal about himself: his feelings of worthlessness, his pent-up anger, his occasional self-destructive urges, and how he could begin to take pride in himself.

Much earlier, Jim's parents might have assisted him in avoiding some of the pain of these difficult years. And Jim's problems might remind all parents that when they feel critical toward their children, it is best to move with caution, to be sure they understand the reasons why they feel so angry or unsatisfied with their children's behavior. Children such as Jim challenge parents who may feel they too have failed—but they need to be sure that their criticism does not reflect their own unfinished business, some trait they dislike in themselves or were unable to deal with in the past.

As parents, adults need to remember that they too may have been victims of similar criticism—and need to be on guard to avoid perpetuating such behavior. Sensing these dangers, parents can mount a dedicated campaign to empathize rather than criticize.

That is, most of all, what children need. With empathy, children often can summon the strength to grow past these disturbing traits. But if parents do forget their own childhood crises and criticize without restraint—as Jim's father did—they run a high risk: that their children will internalize these harsh words—take them inside themselves—and accept criticism as gospel.

Often, children are so vulnerable that they accept parental criticism without question. In Jim's case, it was fortunate that his mother urged him to seek counseling. It was a wise decision, because when Jim reached age seventeen, he did need professional aid.

One of the first questions to come up in therapy was simple enough: What happened in Jim's early life?

Jim recalled without difficulty that even when he was a little boy, he felt he never could do anything right. The demands on him always seemed one or two steps beyond him. And as his fear of failing heightened, it was safer for his fragile ego to avoid *doing*—to avoid trying to learn anything new. Jim was unaware of this defensive process, but it preserved the shrinking self-esteem he had left.

The Parental Role

As a teenager, Jim became as critical of his peers as his parents were of him. He filled the portrait of the typical underachiever: sulking, day-dreaming, procrastinating, often stubborn, inefficient, and rebellious, more likely to express himself passively by failing to act than by taking action.

Underachievers, for instance, will fail to complete assignments and to follow through on chores. They will deeply resent criticism. But they also anticipate failure. Faced with a task or challenge, they do not expect to succeed. At the same time, they become highly critical of others. The reaction of children with intimations of failure is understandable: They put off the frightening challenge, since they believe failure is inevitable, an embarrassing and painful prospect.

How can parents help? First and foremost, they need to examine how they think and feel about their children—and equally important, how they act on those thoughts and feelings. In the home, many roles are played by parents, at times without conscious planning. For instance:

1. *Parents who seek perfection.* Mothers and fathers who have not come to terms with their own lack of perfection can communicate to the children that nothing short of perfection is acceptable to them. But children are not likely to approach perfection—or achieve at all—without taking some risks of failure. They want to please their parents, and they find their parents' disappointment unbearably painful. It is not unusual for these children to choose to do nothing. At least they have not failed.

2. *Parents who lack self-confidence.* Often they react to their own insecurity by pressuring their children to achieve beyond their capacity. In this way, they use their children as their own "second chance."

3. *Parents who are overinvolved.* These parents may substitute their own image of success for their children's achievement. These parents may feel total responsibility for their children's success or failure. Often, the overinvolved parent may be the type of personality who wakes up with a mental "must" list of things to do, the kind of person who seldom feels free to enjoy life.

4. *Parents who feel competitive with their children.* They will find it difficult to tolerate a successful child. They may belittle their children's intelligent questions, frustrate opinions that differ from their own, become angry when a child scores a point in an argument, and insist on having

29

the last word: "Now that's that or you go to you room . . ."
How often have children heard such phrases!

The Child's Inner World

Underachieving children invariably view themselves in a
very negative way. They are also likely to belittle other children, to express hostility toward them, and to be suspicious of
both children and adults. Because of their own poor self-esteem, they find it difficult to believe that other people can
really value them or like them.

They tend to be highly defensive, always ready with an
excuse or an explanation. Their own attitude toward themselves has become one of "not good enough." And even when
they are praised, they still cannot feel "smart enough."

These children often have a great fear of being "ordinary."
Failing to feel exceptional, they feel like total failures. The
issue of accomplishment causes them great anxiety. Such children may respond to this kind of anxiety in two distinctly
different ways:

• By developing an obsessive/compulsive need to please.

• By becoming indifferent to achievement.

For underachievers, the options for action are very limited. They are underachieving because of conflicting emotions.
Thus, "lazy" children are psychologically unable to work effi-
ciently. They have no more conscious control over this lethargy
than over a physical disability. They are silent rebels. Their
angry feelings are unacceptable to themselves, so instead of
saying, "I won't," they say, "I can't."

By resisting success passively, they act in a self-defeating
way. But from their point of view, it is safer to engage in a cold
war with their parents—enabling them to conceal their anger,
and at the same time, to punish their parents.

In effect, these children can make their parents feel frustrated—feelings they may have experienced in the past as a
result of their parents' high expectations and criticism. Here,

once again, it is vital for parents to remember that their children are not conscious of this behavior.

What Parents Can Do

Achievement comes naturally in the development of a child, almost from the time an infant takes its first breath.

An infant tries to roll over for the first time.

A child in a crib reaches for a toy.

A toddler struggles with his first steps.

As witnesses to these first efforts toward success, the warm smiles and enthusiastic applause of parents can add encouragement along the way.

Children are aware of these reactions, and approval of their parents is the reward for their achievements. Later, the achievement itself becomes reward enough for the child. The role of parents in aiding their children to develop this desire to achieve requires exquisite sensitivity, profound patience and self-discipline. Of course, this sounds like a tall order for any human being, but here are some recommended steps:

1. Praise the accomplishments of your children, even the most minor ones.

2. Support their attempts to achieve, even when they are unsuccessful. And try to empathize with their lack of complete success.

3. Allow children to be playful and silly. This may make some parents uncomfortable, but children are naturally more playful than adults, and it is in the play of children that we see the seeds of their future creativity.

4. Allow your children to express their anger. It is, of course, up to the parent to set boundaries and acceptable outlets for these feelings. But when children begin to talk, they should be permitted to speak out, to express their feelings. At an earlier age, substitute targets for anger might be selected. For instance, if a child feels angry at a newborn sibling, parents can provide a doll on which the child can vent his anger safely. In real-life situations, of course, chil-

dren should be restrained if they are about to strike another child.

5. Allow children to make mistakes. Avoid the temptation of belittling your children, which only enrages children and lowers their self-esteem.

6. Be sensitive to traits in your children that remind you of your own doubts and shortcomings. If your children behave in a way that is especially annoying, pause before criticizing them—and explore the possibility that the trait can be found in yourself.

7. Take part in activities with your child that avoid competition or achievement—for example, going to movies, reading books together, taking sightseeing or nature trips, and the like.

8. Do not blame schools automatically when there is a problem with your children. Many underachieving children, for instance, develop a defiant attitude toward authority, and these children will often enrage their teachers.

9. Allow children time and space to initiate conversation and to follow the direction their thoughts travel. Try to be aware of your own urge to correct, lecture, suggest or manipulate at a time when your children are expressing their feelings or thoughts.

10. Avoid overpowering your children in an argument or confrontation. Remember how small and powerless you felt when you were engaged in similar battles with your own parents—and remember that children need to rebel in order to develop a keen sense of their own individuality.

Most of all, try to be available emotionally each day for at least some period of time. Children know when parents are there. Sometimes it means setting aside chores, but it is important just to be there for children during a part of each day.

Remembering

Here are a few other suggestions for parents whose children are underachieving.

Remember that these children are impatient with themselves and their progress. They have trouble accepting the idea that improvement in school work is necessarily a slow process. They have trouble tolerating gradual success, and they need constant reassurance that parents understand their frustration.

Also remember how the educational system works: No matter how supportive and loving you as parents are, children will be buffeted by the expectations of many others—teachers and administrators—who often make demands in a way that is perceived as criticism by the child. As parents, you can act at home to balance and soften these harsh experiences in school.

In Jim's case, his parents might have been more careful in reexamining their own feelings about their son's achievements in school. While Jim was a bright little boy, he was not the academic genius his parents imagined him to be.

Some children might be more socially skilled or better adjusted or enriched by cultural advantages. Often, their common sense, valuable in itself, is mistaken for exceptional intelligence. Often, children are a shade less bright than their parents believe. And so many children are tormented in their school years by their parents' mistaken assumption that somehow they ought to be at the top of their class, no matter what.

It is fine to think that your children are brighter and more beautiful than the children of others. It is not so fine when parents make those notions an unrealistic burden on their own children. Those burdens can diminish rather than heighten a child's chances to move up the ladder of achievement.

Making Sure

Can parents truly assess their child's potential? To begin with, parents may ask themselves:

- "Why isn't my child more interested in school?"

- "Why does my child feel school is such an unhappy place?"

- "Why doesn't my child express his feelings?"

Then, pay close attention to your children's reaction to life at school. If they seem bored or overwhelmed, you might make a special effort to examine the classroom situation and the school.

Is the school environment challenging enough? Is it too much of a challenge? Or is lack of interest a way of avoiding failure? Is failure coming only in some areas and not others, suggesting a possible learning disability?

In many cases, a thorough psychological evaluation, to assess the child's strengths and weaknesses, both emotionally and intellectually, can be a valuable aid to parents and teachers. Children can also be assisted in other ways—by tutors, in special classes, or through a flexible curriculum to encourage and excite their imaginations.

But the ability of parents to encourage free expression of feelings in their children is the decisive chapter in the psychological history of most families.

In Jim's case, his parents unknowingly clamped down on their son's feelings. If he had been more free to reveal himself and his anger, his problems would have been apparent at an earlier age, and Jim might not have acted out his anger through failure in the classroom.

There are limits in expressing anger, of course, and children can learn to express their feelings without verbally abusing their mothers and fathers. To this end, parents can serve as role models. But the same goal remains: the expression of feelings in a socially acceptable form, so that the existence of anger or pain or fear is communicated.

Jim was unable to communicate his angry feelings, and so he turned his anger against himself. He simply shut down—tuned out—to hide his vulnerability and began to punish himself. Driving into a tree, of course, would have been the ultimate punishment.

When Jim told his mother about the accident, she became concerned and urged him to see a therapist. Later, Jim was able to understand that his father's devastating criticism—that nothing Jim did was ever good enough—was a feeling linked to his father's own dissatisfaction with himself. And finally, Jim was able to recognize that his father did not mean to hurt him.

So Jim began to understand how angry he truly was, the long-buried root of his despair, and he took the first steps on the way back to good health and a better relationship with his parents.

MYSTERY ILLNESS

Illness can be a potent instrument for self-defeat.

In the crises of childhood, emotional traumas can take on many unexpected, sometimes astounding, infuriating, and saddening forms. There are many self-defeating patterns that parents encounter in their children—allergies, nail-biting, bed-wetting, and others. Some seem minor, annoying, "a stage," as parents often say.

Other problems are more immediately recognizable but still beguiling and difficult to solve. For both Sharon, who suddenly lost her hearing, and Amy, who developed severe stomach cramps when she began school, traumatic loss and the fear of separation played powerful roles.

There are times, too, when parents unknowingly become the model for the way their children learn to express their emotions. Sharon, for instance, learned early that sick people receive special and loving treatment. Amy responded to her fear of school and the terrifying separation from her mother with her most effective weapon—becoming too sick to leave her home.

Children like Amy can develop health problems such as headaches and other ailments to avoid the trauma of separation. If these patterns are rewarded, the child may continue to express anxieties through his or her body for many years.

Amy and Sharon both suffered during their early lives, and their burden might have been lightened if they had been able to communicate their fear of being separated from their families and homes. If children are encouraged to express this pain and fear to an adult who can comfort them, they would be less likely to express these feelings through their bodies.

Amy: When a mother dies

Amy can recall a painful memory—the arrival of her newborn sister from the hospital. She was only four years old at the time, but she remembers the new baby's arrival with despair.

The memory is blurry: Amy is in the kitchen or in her mother's bedroom. Something is wrong. She cannot remember her mother's face. Perhaps her mother is leaning over a crib. Perhaps she is feeding the baby. But Amy cannot remember what her mother looks like. All she can recall is her mother's back. And Amy does not feel very well.

Another memory Amy has retained probably happened the following year, when she was five: She is alone in her room at night, trying to fall asleep. She is feeling sad because her mother is not home. She does not think about her father or her older brother, only her mother. Again, she cannot remember what her mother looks like. The memory links Amy to the time her mother returned to work, a year after Amy's sister was born.

Amy's mother, Dora, was a pediatrician who practiced in the children's wing of a large hospital. Amy's father was a lawyer. When he returned home in the late afternoon, Dora left for the night shift at the hospital. They had decided to split their working hours so Dora could care for her new daughter during the day and resume her medical career with a residency in pediatrics.

Amy hated it when her mother left the house. When her sister was born, Amy had to live with her grandmother for a week. Later, her mother would come home and talk about the other children, the ones at the hospital. One night, she came in and sat on the edge of Amy's bed and talked about how worried and upset she was about a very sick baby. What a high fever the baby had, she said. Amy wished she was the sick baby that night. Dimly, Amy recalls that sometimes she would wait up for her mother. She would come into Amy's room to kiss her goodnight.

Sometimes Amy was very angry and wished her mother would go away. And her mother did.

A Death in the Family

Amy was ten years old when her mother died.

One night her mother went to work and never came home. On the way to the hospital, she was killed in a car accident. The next morning, her father said that Amy's mother was away on a trip. Later, Amy was told that her mother had died in an accident, but it all seemed so vague. All she knew was that her mother was gone.

Amy's emotional crisis, however, began long before her mother died. To friends of her family and to relatives, of course, everything had seemed untroubled. Amy's father was a diligent parent and a supportive husband, encouraging his wife's new career and working hard to provide material advantages for the family.

His wife had considered herself a good mother, well read on the latest trends in child raising. She was a bit harassed, so busy with a new baby at home and working full-time at night. But Amy and her older brother were so grown-up, she said, playing by themselves, offering to do household chores.

The symptoms of Amy's problems surfaced when she was six years old and there was one jolt too many: Amy had to go off to school.

Without warning, she was taken away from her mother for almost the whole day. While Amy was in school, her mother would be home, tending the new baby. And when Amy returned home, her mother would soon leave for work, looking after the other babies, the ones at the hospital.

Of course, Amy's mother had no idea of her daughter's turmoil. After all, many mothers had to work. And then, Amy was supposed to be in bed by 8 o'clock. She had arranged her work schedule so that she was sure to see Amy in the morning and, at least briefly, after school.

But Amy had her own solution.
She got sick.

The Way Out

In the mornings, as the school bus approached her house, Amy would grow sick to her stomach. Sometimes, she would be gripped by terrible cramps. She had never felt so sick before.

The pains were quite real. Amy was not imagining or faking. Years later, she still recalls the pain and the feeling of panic each morning.

Why was Amy in pain?

Later, in therapy sessions, she discovered how profoundly distressed she was at the thought of losing her mother, a loss she experienced each morning. But at the time, it was an anxiety she neither understood nor communicated. So the turmoil was expressed through her stomach.

Overwhelmed by her anxiety over this abrupt separation from her mother, Amy felt as if she were suffering a little death each day. As she grew older, she hoped the pains wouldn't return, but she was unaware why this terrible experience was happening to her.

Looking back, Amy remembers how upset she was. She would become tense about a half hour before the school bus would arrive, afraid the pains would start again. Then she would beg her mother to permit her to remain home. And, on occasion, her mother did.

But the tension was awful. First of all, the pain was truly terrible. And then, her mother became annoyed with her and the recurring morning routine. So Amy did not get what she wanted most in the world: the sympathy and caring her mother gave so freely to those babies in the hospital and to her sister.

Sometimes, her mother would act as if there was nothing wrong with Amy, as if there was no pain at all. Of course, she had taken her daughter to their family doctor and a series of tests had been done. But they uncovered no organic problems.

At other times, when Amy was allowed to remain at home

39

on a school day, she didn't even get to see her mother. She had to stay in bed in her room while her mother was busy with her little sister. So there was no relief at all: Amy could either go to school and not see her mother or she could stay home and feel just as abandoned. But when she stayed home, at least the pains went away.

Amy felt confused about Katie, her baby sister. She knew her mother really loved Katie, and if she twisted Katie's toe, for instance, Amy knew it would make her mother angry and upset.

Later, as an adult, Amy wasn't sure she ever really did anything to torment Katie, but there is no doubt in her mind that she wanted to. Certainly it was an idea she relished at the time. She really did want to get back at her mother for all the time she spent with her new sister.

During this period, Amy remembers her mother reading Bible stories to her sister and herself.

"God loves everyone," her mother said.

"Not me," Amy thought to herself.

She was about nine years old at the time. The memory came back years later, and it enabled Amy as an adult to understand how much she hated herself and how angry she was at her mother.

A year later, Amy's mother was killed in the car collision. Just as Amy had sometimes wished, she was gone. And in a secret part of her psyche, she felt she was to blame. It was she who had made her mother die. It was being angry that did it. Her wish had come true.

In children, this notion is sometimes called "magical thinking."

It was something Amy was too young to comprehend. She did not understand that her anger could not kill her mother or anyone . . . that it was all right to be angry . . . that she could be angry and still love her mother.

Years before, Amy had watched a train cross a trestle during a family trip one summer through the Rockies. She remembered the scene vividly:

"I thought that if I wished hard enough, the train would

crash down into the gorge. Can you imagine? I thought I actually could make a train crash . . . What a sick kid!"

But Amy's fantasy about the train and her equally vivid sense of guilt about her mother's death are examples of magical thinking—not unusual at all in little children. The trouble with such fantasies can come later—when the event comes true.

Being Sick, Staying Sick

Amy remembers the morning her father told her about her mother—that her mother wasn't coming home again. Her mother was gone! Amy became sick to her stomach.

But what happened? Amy is not sure. Her mother must have died the day after the accident. Amy never saw her. No one told her what really happened. And most important of all, there was no one to whom Amy could express her feelings.

She cannot remember talking about her mother's death with her sister. Her father was having troubles of his own. Feeling depressed most of the time and preoccupied with "keeping the family together," he was working doubly hard to avoid the pain of his loss. So her father was seldom home.

For a time, Amy's grandmother stayed with the family. But Amy could not tell her about her strange feelings of guilt. Magical thinking had become a powerful force for Amy, although it is unlikely that she actually came to terms with the feeling that she was a murderer. The notion rose up only later in therapy.

Amy did recall her mother's funeral. She tried so hard not to feel anything. It was a conscious effort. She stood in the cemetery and did not cry or even sulk. What a brave little girl, people said.

Amy's grandmother stayed with the children for several months. At home, when Amy felt sad, her grandmother would say, "Be a brave little girl." So her lessons were restated: She learned not to cry or to feel angry or sad. And her stomach pains recurred.

After the death of her mother, Amy refused to go to school at first. She stayed home all day, bundling herself up in her mother's favorite quilt, another attempt to become closer to her mother, to bring her back, to keep her alive. At night, Amy stayed up late, watching the little TV set in her room, hours after her father and grandmother went to bed.

Amy was very depressed. She moped all the time. A school psychologist stepped in briefly when Amy refused to go to school. He recommended therapy, and for a short time Amy saw a psychiatrist, who prescribed an antidepressant medication. Amy did begin to attend classes again, off and on, but her underlying problems were never worked through, and her feelings of lethargy remained a daily problem.

A few years after her mother's death, Amy's father remarried and decided to move to a different community. But Amy wanted to remain in the old neighborhood, ostensibly to finish school but where all her childhood memories were stored. So she was invited to stay with an aunt and uncle who lived in the high school district. They were a caring couple, but Amy's stomach problems continued.

As time passed, her physical problems became manageable. Then Amy discovered the piano. It was her first genuine interest since her mother's death, and Amy became quite accomplished. Distracted by her involvement in her music, for a time her depression lifted.

Growing Up

Amy was able to complete high school. Then, after graduation, she enrolled in a community college, planning to switch later to a university as a pre-med student. She decided she wanted to follow in her mother's footsteps.

During exam time, the stomach pains would return, since her body had learned long ago to express anxiety in that way. The pains began to recur with greater frequency and intensity. Often, she would be gripped with pain just before a conference with an instructor or during an interview when she was applying to four-year colleges.

Then a friend suggested that Amy "see a shrink."

Amy was nineteen at the time. Three years passed. While in therapy, Amy entered medical school. The stomach pains gripped her only occasionally. She still fought the old shadowy notion—that she was responsible for her mother's death, although she knew consciously that her feelings of guilt were irrational and unfounded.

In her social life, she was very careful. By age twenty-two, she had experienced few happy emotional relationships. The young men Amy selected were all similar to her father and to her, unwilling and unable to become fully involved. Each time, she would be the one to end the romance. She was not ready to be abandoned again.

Finding Help

In therapy, Amy began to regain her emotional and physical health. By now, her most severe stomach symptoms have ceased.

But years before, Amy's family might have eased her emotional burden. Intervention could have come first when Amy's sister was born. In such situations, there are a number of guidelines parents might keep in mind:

1. Before the birth of a new child, prepare the other children for the event. For many children, the birth of a new brother or sister is often their first separation from their mother.

2. It is more reassuring if children are left with someone who is familiar: their father, a close relative, a neighbor they trust or know well.

3. Familiar surroundings are also best. At home, children are comforted by familiar rooms, by a familiar bed, by the sight of their own toys and games. Such simple things allay their anxiety about this frightening turn of events. At Amy's age, for instance, children really do not have a conception of time—not time as it ticks away in the adult world. So it is not really soothing to say, "Your mommy will be home in only three days," because time can seem

like an infinity to a child. Even those simple words—"only three days"—are meaningless to a small child.

4. Children can be reassured if they have something tangible to hold on to while their mother is gone—a photo, a change purse, an eyeglass case, a knitting bag, anything personal belonging to their absent parent.

5. Telephone calls are always welcome. During a first separation from their mother, children need as much contact as possible with their mother. Some parents might worry that telephone calls from the hospital might upset children and make them cry. But tears are quite appropriate. It is a sad time for the children at home. So it is most important to allow children to express their feelings, to experience their sadness and sense of loss and to discover that they can survive sadness and go on.

Thus, a child learns to be less frightened at the notion of separation, real or imagined, in the future. The process is very different from a more familiar approach, which seems so benevolent: To offer comforting words such as "Don't cry . . . Mommy will be home before you know it."

Such reassurances mean little to a small child. Holding and physically comforting a child is far more meaningful than words. And such gestures go a long way in acknowledging that this period is indeed very difficult for the child.

Later, when Amy's mother had resumed her career, she might have avoided talking to Amy about the other children in the hospital and how upset she was about their illnesses. Her well-meaning words were probably an attempt to share some of her experiences with Amy. But they may have heightened Amy's sense of sibling rivalry. And at the same time, they may have unconsciously prompted the notion that if Amy also was ill, her mother would stay home to take care of her.

But Amy did not communicate her distress until much later. Often, children will give signs of not getting enough attention and affection. Often, they will act out deliberately to annoy their mother, especially if she is busy with a new baby.

Some will regress—begin to wet their beds, to suck their thumbs, to wake up with nightmares, cry for a bottle—long after they had abandoned these baby habits. At times, such behavior will get them the attention the baby is getting. But often, parents will ignore these signals or shrug them off as annoying and unacceptable.

It is best, however, to respond directly and quickly to distress. In such cases, children need comforting, an expression that they are still loved and have not been replaced by a new sister or brother.

Parents need to acknowledge that their children's distressing behavior might be related to feelings of insecurity. They can try to verbalize what their children might be feeling, such as: "Oh, maybe you're feeling bad because I've been so busy with the new baby."

Or when young children become aggressive toward a new brother or sister, parents might provide a doll baby for children to direct their anger safely.

Some parents might say, "Don't feel badly." But it is far less effective to tell children—or anyone, for that matter—not to feel the way they are feeling.

Preparing for Separation

In Amy's childhood, a more clear cry for intervention came when she was sent off to first grade, without any kindergarten preparation.

By the time Amy was six, she had already endured two great losses: the temporary "disappearance" of her mother when her sister was born, and then her mother's return to work the following year.

These separations are part of the reality of modern life. Millions of mothers work full-time or part-time, and parents need not feel guilty about their work lives. But steps can be taken to ease the problems of school-phobic children and to prepare these children to deal with feelings of loss.

Once again, children often do not have the language to express loss, so adults can help youngsters put their sadness and other feelings into words. Parents might say, for example: "You might feel sad at first, when you're in school and Mommy is at work . . . But remember that I'll be thinking about you . . . I'm going to miss you too."

Letting children experience the sadness is more effective than reassuring words—that "you'll have such fun in school."

Amy, for instance, recalls her ambivalence when she first started school. She was very excited by the idea and couldn't wait for the first day of school. After all, her older brother and most of the children on her street went there every day. She really did want to go.

Consciously, at least.

But then, as soon as she would leave for school, anxieties would overwhelm her. When she came home, would her mother still be home? What if she was late from school? What if her mother left early? What would happen? Perhaps these were fears she could not consciously grasp. Amy was only aware of her feelings of anxiety and physical pain.

In Amy's home, expressing anger or sadness was not acceptable or encouraged, so the stomach cramps were a learned response of Amy's body. And after a time, Amy also stopped feeling her anxieties, since her body had learned to express them in terms of physical pain. Thus a self-destructive pattern began, preventing Amy from functioning at full capacity in school.

At age six, it was as if Amy had become stuck, caught in a groove, in an earlier stage of development, where she needed recurring reassurance of her mother's presence every few hours. At age two or three, for instance, young children will play outdoors and will need to step into the house every so often—supposedly for a glass of milk or a cookie—to make sure their mother is still there.

At age six, Amy still needed to check in.

Getting Ready

What can parents do to prepare their children for school?

1. If possible, some experience in a good preschool center or even in the home of a friend without Mother's presence—

for at least a few hours a day—lays the foundation for longer separations.

2. Half-day kindergarten classes also can help a child to bridge the emotional gap.

3. When children beginning school are afraid or under stress, parents should feel free to go with them, for at least a few days. Many schools allow mothers or fathers to stay in the back of the classroom for a time. Parents can remain for a whole morning at first, then for an hour or two daily, until their children make the transition.

4. Parents also feel a sense of sadness and worry when their children start school and leave them for the first time. Children may be sensitive to these feelings, so their parents' fears may make children's adjustment more difficult. For example, if a parent's worry is excessive, a child may react to this unspoken concern by seeing this new adventure as dangerous.

5. Children can take along some personal belongings to remind them of home: a picture of their parents or a favorite toy—things to make them feel more safe in a strange new world. Feeling safe is what it is all about.

When pain and fear are present, they need to be experienced and expressed, in order to be dispelled. But children are terrified that the pain will overwhelm them, that they will fall into a bottomless pit of agony, never to escape. But that is not true. The pain and the fear will pass if the child is supported.

These powerful feelings, however, need to be understood. It is perfectly normal, for instance, for a child to be angry when a parent is sick or dies. But children such as Amy do not know that. They feel guilty when they are angry, and if a parent dies, as Amy's mother did, they can often feel responsible.

In Amy's mind, her wishes made her responsible for her mother's death—her magical thinking at work. Amy suffered unduly because she was unprepared for her mother's death and she was also unable to mourn the loss of her mother.

No one ever told Amy: "It's all right to be angry. Don't feel badly about being angry." In a sad and difficult time, some steps might have been taken to prepare Amy to deal with the death of her mother. Perhaps Amy's father and her other relatives were as eager to deny her mother's death as Amy was. But by refusing to confront their loss, they robbed Amy of the chance to go through this painful experience and then to place it in the past.

Dealing with Loss

In talking with Amy, members of the family might have opened the door gradually to the sad feelings:

"We won't be seeing Mommy and I know you're terribly sad."

"I know you miss her a lot."

"I feel like crying too."

To express these thoughts to a child might be painful and difficult. Amy might have cried often. She would have needed someone to hold her and comfort her while she experienced her terrible sadness. But she could have begun to mourn, to let out some of the pain and, finally, to discover that she was not crushed by it after all.

Many parents forget their own painful experiences as children, and so find it hard to empathize with their offspring. What parents might try to remember, as much as possible, is what it was like for them when one of their parents went away. But many adults have learned to repress such emotions. They instinctively protect their children by encouraging them too to repress their feelings—but that is not serving their children's best interests. Amy paid a high price for such a benevolent impulse.

Sharon: When a friend is lost

Sharon was sprawled on the living room floor, watching television, her head cocked to one side. In the kitchen, her mother Judith was making dinner. At the dinette table, her father Bill was reading a newspaper.

Sharon felt sad. In fact, she had been feeling sad for some time, ever since her grandfather had moved away a month before. Now, in the afternoon, Sharon would come directly home from school and play in front of her house, sitting on the front porch, playing jacks or reading a book. Or if it was rainy, she would play alone in her room.

She never made friends at school, so she was used to playing by herself, walking home from the schoolyard alone, stopping by to visit her grandpa and play cards with him on the front porch for an hour or so.

Then, after her eighth birthday, her grandmother died, and soon after, her grandfather decided to move to Arizona. So Sharon had to invent new games, like solo Monopoly, using all the tokens to represent herself, her grandfather, sometimes her mother or father.

The house felt lonely, even with the TV set on. Sharon's world was growing more and more quiet.

"Sharon!" her mother said, standing in the kitchen doorway. "I've been calling you."

Then she walked into the living room and said again, "Sharon?" She was almost shouting. Sharon barely heard her. In fact, she hardly heard the sounds from the television set.

"I can't hear . . . I can't hear anything at all in my right ear," Sharon said. But she did not cry or complain or seem concerned. Losing her hearing, after all, was a good way of not hearing any more bad news.

Looking for Answers

The next week, Sharon's mother brought her daughter to a number of doctors and finally to an ear specialist for tests. But the medical people could find no reason for Sharon's hearing loss. Then, at a speech and hearing clinic, an audiologist told Sharon's mother that there were apparently no physiological problems in her daughter's case. Suspecting that the roots of the problem were psychological, he recommended a consultation with a psychotherapist. The advice brought immediate relief, at least for Sharon's mother.

In the first session, Sharon's mother told the therapist that her daughter seemed "strange" to her. Sharon seemed different from other children, a loner without friends, constantly arguing with her classmates and the children in the neighborhood. Usually, she either played with children much younger than herself or watched television by herself.

She had been happy that Sharon spent time with her grandfather, sometimes playing cards with him for hours, keeping busy. He was really Sharon's only friend. But it didn't seem healthy.

Sharon's mother just had no idea what to do, she said. And during this private session, she confided that she was glad the therapist was taking over some of the responsibility for the little girl's well-being.

Sharon's mother, a woman in her late thirties, was excessively overweight. She was unable to control her diet, and it upset her. So at home, she made sure that her children didn't overeat or stuff themselves with junk food, the way she sometimes did.

Control was very important to Sharon's mother. One of her fears was that Sharon would turn out to be like Vera. Her older sister Vera could barely control her temper, and on occasion had victimized several members of the family with vicious outbursts of anger.

Sharon's mother did not return to the therapy sessions that followed. Usually, Sharon came in the early evenings with her father Bill, who sat in the park across the street, waiting for Sharon to return.

Bill was a quiet, somewhat withdrawn man who owned an appliance store. His wife, a frugal woman, worked part-time at a local day-care center. With a wife and child to support and a mortgaged house to pay off, Bill saw himself and his family as "good solid people," people who were proud of their middle-class status.

Sharon, their only child, was a nice-looking little girl, just a bit short for her age, polite and formal-looking with her metal-rimmed spectacles. She was always clean and neat, almost too fastidious.

But there was something about the way Sharon looked that seemed out of place. It was hard to identify at a glance. Perhaps it was her clothing, just a bit too large for her, perhaps one size too big. Her mother always bought clothes just a bit too big, since Sharon would grow into them. It was, after all, a way of saving money. That came out later, when Sharon felt more free to voice her complaints about her feelings at home.

She always wanted a pair of trendy jogging sneakers like the other kids, but her mother told her they were too expensive and not practical for school. It was the same with food, Sharon complained. The refrigerator at home was off-limits, and she was always hungry. At her grandfather's house, she had been allowed to have pie or cake in the afternoon. At home, everything seemed to be against the rules.

Escape to Grandpa

In therapy, Sharon talked about her visits with her grandfather. She loved card games, and she knew lots of them.

"Could we play here?" she asked the therapist.

"Of course."

So Sharon showed off all the card games she had learned: war and rummy and casino. The games made it easier for Sharon to begin to talk about her grandfather.

Was she writing to him?

No, Sharon said.

Did she think about him a lot?

No, Sharon said. She didn't remember thinking about her grandfather at all. She would just come home and play by herself. She didn't feel badly or anything.

But slowly, during the card games, Sharon began to talk more openly, and her feelings began to emerge. She was hurt and angry that her grandfather had moved away. He hadn't even told her about the move, not until the last week. And then it was too late to do anything about it.

Now, she guessed, he didn't have time to write to her, and

he would never visit her again. She knew that. She just didn't know why. And it was the same at home. No one cared about her. She just lived there, but she wasn't very important to anybody. Her father often worked late at the store, and her mother was away too, busy with this or that community activity in the evenings.

Sharon didn't feel bad, she said. And no wonder. She was expressing all her painful and sad emotions through her body instead of feeling them. But soon, Sharon grew a little more sure of herself, strong enough to endure some of these painful feelings. She was on the way back. She began to regain her hearing.

What Silence Bought

When Sharon's grandfather moved away, Sharon had felt a terrible void in her life. No friends replaced her loss. At the time, Sharon desperately needed someone to talk to, to express her feelings. It was a situation with which she could have coped, if she had been able to express her feeling of being abandoned by her grandfather.

Instead, there was silence. And her loss of hearing enabled Sharon to shut out the world, at least temporarily, as her body responded to the crisis. In Sharon's case, as in many others, empathy might have been the key to early intervention. Parents might try to recall how they felt as children, about the losses they experienced.

Members of her family had also served as role models of a sort. When she was growing up, Sharon remembered that her uncle once broke his ankle and stayed home for weeks, watching television. Later, an aunt suffered a fall on an icy sidewalk and hurt her back. Her husband would prepare her favorite meals for her. To Sharon, the lesson was clear: Disability meant special treatment.

Was Sharon copying these patterns? Perhaps. Later, Sharon was able to talk about her grandmother's death the year before. That too was traumatic. It became clear that now, her latest loss, her grandfather's decision to move out of state, had set off some old and painful feelings. And Sharon didn't want to hear such bad news any more.

Roots of Trouble

Sharon's family was far from uncaring. Neither mean nor punishing, her mother and father were wrapped up in a complex set of problems of their own, financial and emotional. They were unaware that Sharon had been on a collision course with crisis long before her grandfather moved away.

Because Sharon was so verbal and a bit of a fuss-budget, she was often teased at school. And her defenses inspired even more torment. Refusing to show her wounded feelings, she would lash back at her tormentors, demeaning their intelligence with her sharp tongue.

In her own mind, Sharon knew she was smarter than most of these enemies. She didn't need them. They were dumb, she said later. So she hated it when her parents forced her to join in school activities or the Girl Scouts. Sharon didn't need anyone. She would rather go home to read. Or she could always visit her grandfather.

In therapy, it became clear that Sharon had a wonderful mind. She would read history books and talk at length about complex plots in novels. She loved stories about castles and knights and their ladies. She remembered everything she read. And her scores on intelligence tests were not surprising. Sharon placed in the range of "very superior," occupied by about two percent of the population.

But a high IQ is no defense against monsters. They would appear in her dreams and show up in the artwork she did in therapy.

Finger-painting was a good start. At first, Sharon hated the idea of getting her hands and her clothing "dirty." She was afraid her mother would be angry if she spilled paint on her dress. But she was reassured that if she wore old clothes, no one would scold her. And she discovered that paint does come off afterward.

She was tentative in the early sessions, dipping into the

paint pots as if she were picking up some distasteful toad out of a fairy tale. And her early creations were constricted. But later the pictures became more expressive, darker, more aggressive. Some faces represented her most dreaded schoolyard enemies.

Often, she would X-out their faces. Later, she invented other monster-drawings, who came to her aid in her fantasy wars. When she allowed herself to let go, her aggression was rampant. Anger leaped out of her drawings: pictures of clowns with daggers through their hearts, cars running down victims, other flashes of violence. She painted with ardor and later, as she felt better, her hearing began to return.

In talking about the drawings, Sharon related them to her mean enemies at school and to her mother. Sharon said she was angry at her mother all the time. Her mother was always talking, always telling her what to do:

"No more dessert."

"Wash your face."

"Tidy your room."

"Act like a lady."

So she stopped listening. She shut out the bad news in the world, like her grandfather's decision to move away. And it also silenced the endless criticism of everything she did.

Facing Another Loss

While Sharon was relieved when her hearing returned, she was not sure she should admit that everything was perfectly fine. Even later, she claimed she still had "a little trouble hearing," although hearing tests showed a full recovery. Most likely, she was not ready to admit that she was completely cured—to risk losing her new relationship with her therapist, just as she had lost her grandfather.

At home, after all, there was still tension. Sharon continued to feel neglected. Once her father found an old bike and repainted it for her. When Sharon first saw it, she was happy. But then, a moment later, when she realized it was not a new bike, she felt sad: She never received any new toys the way her friends did. Unable to appreciate her father's gesture—painting a bike especially for her—Sharon felt as if she was not special enough to deserve something better.

Later, her mother blamed herself. Perhaps she was too afraid Sharon would grow up with some of her failings. Sometimes, Sharon's mother said, she was terribly afraid of losing control, of eating too much, of yelling too much. They were fears she had recognized recently. Perhaps that was why she was so upset when Sharon expressed anger and sadness. Yes, Sharon's mother said, she would try to ease her hold on her daughter.

During this period, there was another death in the family, Sharon's Aunt Martha. After her grandfather had moved away, Sharon's aunt had become a surrogate pal. After school, she began to stop by her aunt's. She was very old, but Sharon liked to talk to her. When the old woman died, Sharon's mother wondered if her daughter should attend the funeral. She was nine years old at the time.

Sharon's mother was horrified at the idea that a little girl like her daughter should have to go through such a sad afternoon. But after talking with her daugter's therapist, she became convinced that Sharon should join the family and be allowed the opportunity to feel and express her grief.

Sharon did attend the service and later, for the first time, she talked about her feelings, almost eagerly. She felt very sad, but she was also very curious. Would she ever see her aunt again? Would her grandfather die too? What was death? She said she was keeping her aunt's picture on the top of her dresser. And in her own way, she was coming closer to truly experiencing loss.

Helping Sharon

Sharon's parents had always wanted to protect their daughter. By not talking about the departure of Sharon's Grandpa Charlie or the death of Sharon's aunt, they felt they could shelter her. Certainly they felt they were doing what was best. But then, it was the way they dealt with almost everything: with silence.

Before Sharon's grandfather had moved to Arizona, for instance, Sharon's parents might have begun the groundwork for the move, to ease the wrenching separation Sharon felt but would keep to herself.

Several approaches might have eased Sharon's sense of loss:

1. Her parents might have explained in detail why her grandfather was leaving and where he was going.

2. They might have planned weekly letter-writing sessions.

3. A visit in the near future might have been discussed, an adventure for the whole family.

But Sharon's parents were not aware how deeply their daughter felt the loss of her grandfather. Parents are often unaware how devastating such a loss can be for a small child—and how the hurt can be soothed if it is dealt with directly. Sharon might have accepted the reality of loss if she had not been caught so off balance, emotionally—feeling suddenly alone, as if there had been a death in the family.

"We know it's sad," her parents might have said, "we know you are really going to miss Grandpa." Instead, there was silence, an emotional cover-up that failed.

As therapy progressed, Sharon became much happier, although she still had difficulty making friends. And while she was still angry, she was able to talk about her pain more freely. Less preoccupied with her grandfather's absence, she became more interested in school activities. She was coping for the first time with her realities, even though she was still lonely.

"Do you like any of the kids at school?" the therapist asked her.

"No," she said, "not now."

"Gee, you seem to know so many mean people. Do you know any nice ones?" the therapist asked.

"Well," Sharon said, "yeah, maybe you."

It was a beginning.

Crisis
IV

TROUBLE WITH SEX

For many parents, the sexual experiments of children can evoke fury, tears, or silence. The sexuality of an adolescent, just a child a few years before, is difficult for some parents to accept.

Parents are often uncomfortable. Traditional notions of parenting rise out of the ashes of the past. Even "liberal" parents become hand cuffed by old moral taboos. Questions are difficult to ask. Answers are complicated.

Does the sexual behavior of their adolescent reflect anger? Depression? Escape? Revenge? Or is it natural—a signal of impending adulthood that mothers and fathers may be unready to recognize?

We will examine these questions and suggest how parents can keep up a dialogue with children they feel are growing up too fast. There are roles to be played by mothers and fathers, even if they do not condone their adolescent's exploration of sexuality. There are exchanges of ideas that can be made. There are doors that can be left open, at least symbolically.

With or without parental sanction, teen sexuality is a fact of life. And there are differences between dangerous sexual acting-out and healthy experiment. There are also elements of anger and depression, expressed in disguised ways, that can take parents by surprise.

Masochism, for instance, can play a role in disguise. Adolescents may select sexual adventures as a way of punishing

57

themselves for a variety of reasons—often unknown to parents and rooted in their past sorrows and deeply buried antagonisms.

So it was with Dana, who deeply missed her father, absent since he and Dana's mother had ended their marriage years before. But there are others—teenagers like Ronni and Kit—who decided at an early age that they were old enough to test their sexuality in adult fashion. They were adolescents and still vulnerable to the pain of parental abandonment. But their sexual reality needed recognition too.

Dana: An early abortion

Dana felt that her life wasn't worth living. For more than two years, she had been miserable. Now, sitting at the desk in her bedroom, she stared at a sheet of stationery in front of her.

The lives of other people flashed before her eyes: people who committed suicide in movies and in books. They wrote such graceful and heart-breaking notes of farewell. But Dana couldn't think of anything to say. Finally she wrote:

"Dear Mother . . . Goodbye."

It was mid-afternoon. Her mother would be home later, in the early evening. Her father would not be coming home at all. He lived in Denver, and Dana had not seen him for almost a year. She wouldn't even mention him in the note. He'd know the reason.

Then she opened up a small bottle of sleeping pills. Very deliberately, she counted them out. How many would it take? She didn't know. She hadn't planned this very well. She lined up twenty pills and spelled out a letter: "T" for Tom.

She took out a pile of photos of Tom, her boyfriend, and very slowly cut them into small pieces. Then, with a can of diet soda, she washed down the twenty pills, one by one. Sitting down on her bed, she stared at the wall. She did not feel like crying. She never did. Not even the day before, when she had had an abortion.

It was not the first time. Two years ago, when she was

fifteen years old, she had the first one. That was just a few months after she had met Tom.

Now, at seventeen, Dana tried to remember if she had ever felt so bad. Never, she thought. In fact, she seldom felt depressed or angry about anything. After all, life was a process of being hurt, wasn't it? Even when she was a little girl, a soundless voice had told her life was that way.

Then she had met Tom. It was late summer after her sophomore year in high school. At first, Dana's girl friends viewed Tom as "a great catch." He was nineteen. Nice looking. Had a job at a hotel and lived in his own apartment. He was cool. Not the faithful type perhaps.

Tom was Dana's only sexual partner. But their relationship had been on-and-off for two years. Now, Dana had just completed high school and was planning to enter college in the fall. But just a few days after the commencement exercise, Dana confirmed the fact that she was pregnant again.

She had never thought about birth control. Somehow, Dana did not feel she was involved with sex. Tom certainly didn't love her. At least, she didn't feel loved—except when she was being held and hugged. Then, at least for the moment, she did not feel so lonely.

So for two years she had been devoted and loyal, even though Tom let her know that, now and then, other girls would be invited to spend the night with him. For Dana there was no one else. Perhaps there would never be anyone else again.

And whenever she tried to break off their relationship, she failed. Tom would call her a week later and she would return unable to refuse. Or if he made no move, she would call him.

"Can I come over?" she would ask.

"Sure," Tom would say.

And they were together again.

But a persistent feeling of powerlessness shadowed her. Occasionally, Tom would dare her to try cocaine or speed or quaaludes—demands he knew would upset her. Each time, she managed to reject the idea. In Tom's mind, her decision really was not very important. But Dana always ended up apologizing for her decisions.

"I'm always saying I'm sorry," she thought to herself. But Dana also felt guilty for not pleasing Tom. Of course, she felt, it was her fault that he was not more loving with her.

Then came Dana's second pregnancy. This time she did not hesitate at all. She could not have a child at this point in her life. Dana called Tom at work to tell him that the abortion was over. She was all right, she said. That night, she called him again. Perhaps he might take care of some of the expenses. Would he pay half the cost?

Tom refused. "How do I know whose kid it was?" he said.

Dana hung up. Her mother was at work. She was alone and her head was spinning. Maybe she would move to Denver and live with her father. No, that wasn't possible. When would her mother return? She wasn't sure. Since her father and mother had split up, when she was a little girl, there had never been a predictable schedule around the house. Dana wasn't complaining. It saved a lot of energy in arguments with her mother.

Help Long Overdue

Dana woke up in the hospital. Her mother happened to come home early that afternoon. The doctors were able to pump out Dana's stomach but, they told her mother, Dana was not fooling about suicide.

When she came home, Dana was glad to be alive. For the first time, she felt something new: She had scared herself. She felt that she had gone berserk, and the loss of control terrified her. So, for the first time, she asked a psychologist at school for advice. He recommended professional therapy, and Dana began to examine her life and almost-death. The close call with the sleeping pills had been too shocking for Dana to handle alone.

Such experiences raise painful questions for both adolescents and their parents. Why, for instance, did a bright and attractive young woman cling to a painful and unrewarding relationship with a young man who was unconcerned about her welfare, denied her loving support in a crisis, and often made her feel invisible? Why did she place such little value on herself? Why did she expect so little from men?

Some of these questions link Dana's adolescent traumas to much earlier experiences in her life—some just barely conscious, some lost in a maze of anxieties. Long before Dana survived a near-fatal crisis, someone might have helped her.

No one really understood how isolated Dana felt, as if she were living in the middle of an emotional desert, she said later. But Dana's mother and father, like many adults, were beset with problems of their own. Like many caring parents, they felt overwhelmed and unable to cope with family problems, not knowing where or how to start. Years later, Dana's mother admitted: "I just didn't know what to do."

By that time, in therapy, Dana had begun the exploration of her inner world and began to grapple with some of her most painful childhood experiences.

From the Past

When Dana's parents split up, she was just eight years old. Their decision came without warning, and Dana was devastated. She was also furious with her mother. After all, it was her mother who made the decision to move out. Even so, Dana felt guilty, as if she too had abandoned her father.

Dana was an only child, but she always envied the boys who lived on her street. They all seemed much more important than girls were, and she loved to play with them. The boys, most of them older than Dana, were unrestrained in their teasing.

For Dana that memory was vivid, more so than any other fragment of her childhood. Often, the boys would dare her to do the most frightening stunts, such as climbing trees or exploring caves in the woods or swimming across a wide lake during summer vacations. Dana followed them in silence, even when she was terrified. She was afraid that if she protested, they would reject her. Then she would have no one to play with at all. So the casual torment became a tradition that Dana endured for years, into her adolescence.

Looking Back in Despair

Much later, Dana discovered that her childhood experiences had shaped her feelings about herself and about men:

That men were all-powerful and in control.

That she was weak, frightened, needy, neglected, abandoned, . . . and a baby.

She cried when she talked about it.

During her childhood, she remembered, her father was the only person on whom she depended. She loved to be hugged. He always brought little gifts when he came home from the mysterious outside world. Sometimes she felt that she was much more important to her father than her mother was. And she wished that he was home all the time. Then, one day, without any preparation, he was suddenly gone from her life.

There was no warning, because Dana's mother and father wanted to protect her. But their silence did not have that effect. Dana felt that it was she who was leaving her father, at home by himself, with no one to care for him.

Other memories, of course, were blocked out. It was years later when Dana recalled that her parents often argued in the kitchen. Those memories of conflict were still terrifying. After her father and mother split up, all she remembers are feelings of sadness and guilt and anger.

As Dana moved into adolescence, she explored new freedoms. She preferred to stay overnight at the homes of her girl friends rather than staying with her mother. Without her father, home was depressing.

By age fifteen, she was allowed to come in as late as she pleased. Her mother did not seem to worry and set no strict rules. No one told Dana when to study or when to go to bed or whom to date. Not that Dana did anything outrageous or dangerous. She just did what she wanted to. She was free to come and go as she pleased. The trouble was, Dana never felt good about being free.

In Therapy

In an early stage in therapy, Dana discussed Tom and her attraction to boys who were distant and rejecting. Dana was not sure why it happened that way, but it never surprised her. It was, after all, a familiar pattern. Once she saw Tom walking down the street with his arm around a girl, a classmate of Dana's.

"I remember I felt nothing. I don't know why. I felt somehow like I was the one who was guilty. Mostly, I felt numb."

Despite her surface acceptance, Dana's anger had been raging underneath for many years. Then came her final crisis with Tom: her abortion and her suicide attempt, a signal of how much subterranean anger was turned in on herself.

This time, when she lost control, she sought professional counseling. Losing her ability to fend off her self-destructive feelings, Dana was suddenly afraid she was going crazy. It was her first step back on the road to well-being.

She focused at first on her unhappy relationship with Tom. It was purely physical, but the word "sexual" seemed almost out of place, because the only way Dana knew how to be close to anyone was through physical contact. Even at the time, she was aware that "having sex" was not something she enjoyed.

She had felt a physical closeness with her father years before, and it seemed healthy enough when she was a child, loving to be hugged. With Tom, she never really felt any sense of passion. Once again, she felt like a little girl.

Sex just happened. But for Dana, like many teenagers, it was a special kind of intimacy—an attempt to re-create the intimacy she missed with her father. And since Dana never thought about sex, she had no conscious worries about getting pregnant. After all, this really wasn't sex at all. In fact, she felt virginal. Unknowingly, Tom played a convenient role in Dana's fantasy world: He reaffirmed her underlying feeling that she ought to be punished.

Why Be Punished?

Deep down, Dana had her own long list of personal failures.

Hadn't she abandoned her father when she was eight years old?

Hadn't she hated her mother at times, picturing her as a rival for her father's love and attention?

Hadn't she really felt that she was more important to him than her mother was?

To Dana, these feelings were wrong. And Tom confirmed her worthlessness. He also provided another link to her early childhood. She recalled playing with the boys in the neighborhood, and with Tom she reenacted that scenario—allowing herself to be victimized by a young man because she was afraid she would lose her playmate. So she contained her anger. Depression became a familiar coverlet.

Underneath, Dana was in great pain.

Feeling Again

After the incident with the sleeping pills, Dana ended her relationship with Tom. Just the thought of him repulsed her. And after graduation from high school, she continued to live at home and worked at a local bookstore.

Remaining at home, she felt she was still a little child. Her life was going nowhere, and that was just fine: She felt she didn't deserve anything better.

For six months, Dana went into hiding. She saw almost no one. She dated no one. She read or studied constantly. And she discovered that being alone made her feel less lonely than being with Tom. So her life began to take on a new shape. Slowly, she began to discard the idea that a physical relationship was the only way she could feel close to anyone—the way she had felt close to her father as a child.

Dana began to make a connection between her relationship with Tom and her feelings about her father. She began to understand how hurt she had been by the "disappearance" of her father when she was eight years old . . . how she felt that her father had withdrawn his affection at a crucial time in her life. Her father had not meant to hurt her, but from that point on, she had felt deprived.

She became aware, in therapy, that she was afraid to cry or to show anyone how she really felt. The only way she ever could be comforted was physically, she felt. Words were never enough. But Dana began to talk about her father, and new details emerged.

When her parents split up, her father had expressed great concern about Dana. He had called her almost every other day. Often, she spent vacations and holidays with him. Sometimes, he would let her practice cooking dinner for him. It made her feel very grownup. Then, when she was about twelve, he really disappeared. Or at least it felt that way to Dana.

Her father remarried and moved to a city in the Northwest. His move came at a very confusing time for Dana. By then she was taller than her mother. People told her she was very pretty. But in the morning, when she stared at herself in the mirror, she was not sure who was there. At times, she felt womanly. At other times, she felt like a little girl. Would she ever grow up? she wondered.

She really missed her father. By now, telephone calls from him had all but stopped. There were only infrequent letters. His visits were unpredictable, and Dana never knew when he would arrive or depart. Sometimes he would disappear for months at a time.

Even so, Dana never made any demands. She never said:

"How come you don't call me?"

"Why don't you visit?"

"How come you've moved so far away?"

Through it all, she never felt angry, just hurt. If she got angry, he might disappear forever. It was the same feeling she had had when she played with the boys in the neighborhood as a child.

Reading the Signs

When children do not express feelings openly, it can be difficult for parents to understand the inner world of their sons and daughters. With such children, there are important questions that can be asked casually to get conversation rolling. Are they feeling sad? Do they miss their father? What do they like about school?

Dana's mother was too troubled to ask the questions. Three years passed, and that spring, Dana met Tom. A few months later, she became pregnant—and she made sure her mother knew about the abortion.

Dana was almost three months pregnant before she admitted to herself that she was facing a major decision. The process of denial is a familiar one among teenagers. Later, she explained: "I knew I was gaining weight. Knew my clothes weren't fitting. I guess I didn't realize how much time was passing. I felt it was just a few weeks since my last period. But I didn't really think about it."

For Dana, there was an emotional overlay: When she was eleven, she found out that her mother was already pregnant— with Dana—when she was married. It was hardly scandalous, but Dana never mentioned the gossip, overheard on a visit to an aunt's house.

By the time Dana faced the fact that she too was now pregnant, her mother had noticed the change in her daughter's figure and insisted that Dana go for a pregnancy test. With mixed feelings, Dana chose to have an abortion.

For a fifteen-year-old, it was a jarring crisis, but it provided Dana with some unexpected emotional gains. Her mother, for instance, became more worried and protective. And deep down, Dana may have been punishing her mother, without consciously understanding the feeling. After all, it was her mother who drove her father away.

And it was fair too, since Dana was also punishing herself, by feeling guilty about her abortion. What kind of awful person would abort her child? In silence, Dana tortured herself with the idea. Later, talking about it in therapy was a great relief.

A year after counseling sessions began, Dana began to become interested in other men, although she kept them at a distance. Most of them fit an old pattern: men who were emotionally unavailable, like Tom and her father. But the pattern became clear as therapy continued.

As time went on, Dana also discovered that she liked her father's new wife. But at times she felt sad. In her father's new world, she felt she had been replaced. She could no longer recapture her childhood feeling that she was the central figure in her father's life. During a visit with her father, Dana was able to face this painful reality. But she also felt that her father did need her—as a daughter.

Dana, of course, was not free yet. For a long time, she remained angry with her mother, blaming her for the early upheaval in her life. In Dana's inner world, her father and her mother had occupied center stage. After Tom, she was afraid of being hurt in a one-sided relationship, so she often turned down second dates or kept relationships casual. But in therapy, she found support for the first time—the satisfaction of being emotionally close to another human being. The groundwork for future relationships had begun.

Stepping in Earlier

What could have been done? In Dana's case, intervention might have been possible if the early warning signals were spotted. For example:

- Dana's fear of losing the companionship of her playmates. Dana did voice her fears, but she was a timid and compliant child, and her fears were understated. With children like Dana, parents have to be fine-tuned to hear the cries of pain.

- Her fear of losing her father's affection. When a family is confronted with a marital breakup, there is a special need to be on guard for the pain that separation causes a child. In Dana's case, the pain was intensified when her father remarried and moved to another state.

- Her intense feelings about her father. Her focus seemed to exclude all others, including her mother. At age eight, for instance, she seemed to endure the traumatic endgame of her parents' marriage. But in her own mind, her father had vanished. Yet Dana was unable to communicate this sense of loss and fear.

In such cases, parents might act to get their children's

feelings into the open. Even voicing these worries might help to break the block of silence:

"Your friends must really scare you sometimes? . . . Maybe you feel you have to do everything people tell you, don't you? . . . Maybe you're upset when you have no one to play with." But Dana's mother and father found it difficult to detect these early ripples of trouble.

Dana, after all, was successful in school. Low-keyed and often aloof, perhaps, and a bit of a loner, but there was no acting-out during her early adolescent years. Dana did not smoke or drink or get into the drug scene. Outwardly placid, she kept her anger and pain to herself.

Even while feeling hostile toward her mother, she stayed close to home, because she was so afraid of being alone. Trying to act adult with Tom, Dana still had not developed any real sense that she could trust her own judgment, her own power to survive alone. Though she had more freedom than most of her friends, Dana did not feel more self-confident. She had been free to come and go as she wished, but emotionally she was free to go nowhere.

The Future

The problems in Dana's home were not unusual. Often, when a marriage is in trouble, parents feel overwhelmed by anger and disappointment, and communication with their children breaks down. Anger crackles in the air or lurks in the corner.

In Dana's case, her father turned to her briefly—after his separation—as a source of comfort, without a real awareness of Dana's own needs or fears or fantasies. A close relationship was something Dana's father needed and one that Dana romanticized. But this is too heavy a burden for a small child to carry.

So it is important for parents to define clearly the boundaries of their relationships with their children.

Parents, for instance, can protect their children from painfully unrealistic expectations. Often, these feelings affect families in which estranged parents have no adult partner. And even in two-parent families, adolescent thoughts and feelings about an incestuous romance with a father or mother are not unusual, though parents may be unaware they even exist. Children need to be protected from these wishes, not blamed for them.

Spending time with her father was satisfying for Dana during her unsettling pre-adolescent years. But it would have been more healthy if Dana's father had invited one of her friends to join her on those vacation visits—to blunt her fantasy that she was the central female in his life. Dana wished that she was closer to her father, but she would have felt more protected from her own fantasies by the presence of a school friend.

Often after a marital breakup, parents need to engage in some deep soul-searching: Is their nurturing designed to comfort their child or to combat their own loneliness? Often a parent will say, "Oh, my little boy is so lonely because his father isn't around." And the mother will allow her ten-year-old son to spend the night in her bed. Perhaps she also benefits from such closeness, but this arrangement is not beneficial for the child. It can be a painful decision, but it is one that should be faced.

Caring

Dana grew up without any sense of parental structure to bump up against, no feeling of how far she could stray. The effect made her feel uneasy rather than free. The message Dana heard was not: "You're okay . . . We feel you can judge things for yourself." Instead, Dana simply felt: "No one cares."

Clearer rules of behavior might have eased her feelings of abandonment, since self-confidence does not come easily for adolescents. It is attained by leaping a series of hurdles set by parents and other authority figures. And as the barriers are lowered by parents, confidence increases.

Thus a parent can say: "You can go out now but I want you to be home by 6 o'clock." The message is: "I care."

Talking to adolescents, of course, can be a test for the most glib conversationalist. How do you break the conversational ice?

Try to avoid criticism and blame.

Empathize with your child's feelings, to keep the talk door open and not put him or her on the defensive.

Recognize that intellectual understanding will not supply automatic solutions. Behavior changes slowly, and conversation needs to be gentle and tentative.

If all else fails, a father or mother might suggest: "I know it's hard for you to talk to me, but maybe you'd like to talk to a counselor?"

No matter what you say, childen might continue to mope, to be sad or lonely. But it pays to remain attuned to recurring patterns, even when it is tempting to shrug off setbacks with the thought that this is just another sign of "growing up," another bit of adolescent bad luck.

Very often, children will not volunteer information if pressed. But parents should be available. And they can be quite obvious about it, just to get the point across:

"You seem kind of sad."

"You sure look down in the dumps lately."

"I'm here, if you want to talk to me."

Don't push too hard. For many adolescents, talking to parents is difficult, especially if the lines of communication were not opened years before. Adolescents are quick to reply, "It's none of your business," even when parents are trying to be supportive.

Being available emotionally is the key. And you may have to send the message a dozen times before it is received. And even if you have been able to have good talks during pre-adolescent years, you may have to work hard at reestablishing communication during the difficult years of adolescence, when talk often stops and anger roars to the surface.

Ronni: Love and sex

At sixteen, Ronni had the giggle of a school girl and the figure of a young woman. Bright, pretty, and college-bound, she had been involved in a sexual relationship for almost a year.

Like thousands of teenagers who are seventeen or younger, Ronni was "on the pill," despite the consciousness of side effects which has escalated during the past fifteen years. "It's safer than getting pregnant right now," she said. And like her counterparts across the country, Ronni had not shared her secret—about sex or the pill—with her parents.

Instead, she went to an adolescent clinic at a local hospital, a new development in community health care during the past decade. At the time, Ronni was about one of a hundred teenagers who came to the clinic every six months for a medical exam and a half-year's provision of birth control pills.

Ronni made her first visit to the clinic that summer. She had turned sixteen in the spring and had just begun her first sexual relationship with her then-steady boy friend, a freshman at college.

"My mother had told me all about birth control but my boy friend and I, we didn't use anything. The idea seemed so . . . unspontaneous. And every once in a while, I told myself: I'm not going to get pregnant." But near the end of August, Ronni thought something was wrong.

"I thought I was going to die. I was in a panic. You don't know what to do when you're only sixteen and you think you're pregnant. When I told my boy friend, he was furious at me. We'd never talked about doing anything, about taking any precautions. Suddenly he made it seem like it was all my fault."

A senior at her school suggested a pregnancy test. And Ronni made an appointment that day.

"God, what a relief. It came back negative. I wasn't pregnant. But that's when I found out I could do something about birth control myself. When I talked about my experience with my friends, I found out that's the way most kids really learn about birth control—by accident."

Ronni came from a well-to-do suburban background. Her parents were eager to have her attend a good college, and they were reasonably open about sex with their daughter. But Ronni at sixteen was not ready to talk about sex and love with her parents. The secret, however, did emerge soon after. During a hectic argument with her mother, Ronni made an inadvertent confession.

"I got so mad, I just blurted it out, that I wasn't a virgin. I didn't mention anything about birth control. I think the stuff about sex came out because I wanted to hurt her. You know, show her I was independent. But I also felt relieved—that I wasn't going behind her back anymore. I felt more adult. But the big surprise came the next morning when my mother told me that now she was sorry—that I had told her anything at all. She said: 'For God's sake, don't tell your father.' She just wanted to drop the whole subject."

Ronni laughed. "I'm still my father's little girl, you know."

The issue of sex and the pill was put on hold. Ronni decided not to mention birth control, she said, because her mother would have been even more upset. "She probably would have thought it meant I had sex all the time."

About her first sexual relationship, Ronni had some serious reservations. "It really wasn't my idea, but he kept talking and talking and talking about it all the time. He wouldn't leave me alone, so finally I said okay, all right. Also I think I was curious and pretty turned on. I thought I was madly in love, and like most of my friends at school who had boy friends, I didn't want to lose him."

Then the pregnancy scare came. It set off a series of recurring fights that Ronni was not prepared to handle, and it ended the relationship. But reflecting on the crisis later, Ronni said, "I don't think I really knew him very well, but I thought I was really in love." She paused and added: "Actually, I don't think I really liked him very much."

Kit and Caution

It might have been cute graffiti on a high school wall, a suburban sidewalk, an occasional tree:

"Kit loves Ray."

But it was true. Kit did love Ray. And since she was fifteen, she had also slept with her boy friend. Not often. But often enough, she said.

She did not like the phrase "sexual intercourse." It

sounded too scientific, too much like one of those phrases out of a textbook or a teen survey. For Kit, sex was an act of love. It was neither a disaster nor a messianic event. And for Kit, for her older sister, and for most of her eleventh grade friends, their first entry into the adult world of sex occurred just before or just after their sixteenth birthday.

Kit's sister had actually talked with their mother after her first sexual experience with her boy friend. "Oh my God, you're just a baby . . . What do you know about anything?" her mother exclaimed, feeling angry and excluded. Kit decided to avoid her sister's unpleasant experience.

She also recalled that one of her friends, who was fifteen at the time, had been on the living room couch with her boy friend, watching television, when her father walked in and discovered them, half-clothed. "If I ever see you again, I'll kill you," the girl's father shouted at her boy friend, breaking up the romantic session for the evening.

They slept together for the first time the next week—at the boy's house. Parents, Kit said, were like ostriches. All of them. All the parents who don't want to know what's really going on. All the parents who think nobody's doing anything—at least not their daughter. "All these parents who think that if you are having sex, you're one of the school sluts and you're doing it all the time," she said.

At sixteen, Kit saw herself as "average" within her school community. She did well in class, and was full of high spirits and self-esteem. She had gone out with her boy friend Ray for two years, since she was thirteen and he was fourteen. "We never did anything." Until the relationship broke up a year later, he had been her only sexual partner. And their sexual encounters were certainly less than prodigous.

"Maybe we did it four or five times a month," she recalled later. "Most of all, it was real emotional, it was very spiritual. I mean it," she said. "I didn't think sex was dirty or anything like that. I was really in love and I wanted him to be happy. I never worried about getting a reputation. You got one anyway, sometimes, even if you did nothing. If you go steady with a boy for a couple of months, then most kids at school just assume you're having sex anyway."

Yet Kit and most of her school friends limited their sexual experiences to one boy.

"At least until senior year," Kit said. "I had one good friend who didn't sleep with anyone in high school. She just didn't find anyone she really cared about enough." Then, she said, there are always some girls who "do it with everybody." According to updated double standards, these were the girls with the "reputations," Kit said. Her own friends demanded that sex had to be emotional and romantic.

"It had to be special," she said. And at the time, it had to remain a secret at home.

Kit had matured early, both physically and intellectually, but she lingered on the sexual threshold long after she was aware of sexual feelings.

"One of my friends was really used by a boy and I didn't want that to happen to me. So I was just friends with a lot of boys when I was thirteen and fourteen. All I wanted was to have fun. But I also wanted to care about someone."

She started to see Fred as her special boy friend when she was fourteen. They would hang out at each other's house. Lie on the floor. Listen to music. Go to the beach in the summer.

"We didn't even start to pet until after I was sixteen. We never really decided to make love. It just happened, one night after a party, at her boy friend's house, when his parents were away . . . I was glad it happened. I loved him so much. I felt very good about it. Not guilty at all."

Sexual activity was slightly more frequent during their first month of lovemaking. "Maybe it happened five or six times. Once in Central Park. That was on a dare. It was crazy. . . . But we really loved each other then. After that, it would happen two or three times a month, when we really missed each other."

Kit, who is now in her twenties, thought for a moment.

"I think sex was like a pie. If you have too much at one time, you get a stomach ache. If you have just a little bit, there's more left for later . . . In the back of my mind, I think there was something puritanical, something most girls have, that maybe he won't like me anymore, after I sleep with him."

The feeling had flitted about in the corner of her mind, she recalled.

But she never worried about getting pregnant. "Most of us left it up to the boy. There were a lot of girls who didn't want to try the pill and mess around with chemicals. Or else they were afraid their parents would find them. Anyway, almost no one knew you could even get the pill without your parents knowing about it."

So Kit just put the idea of getting pregnant out of her mind. Later, when she was in college, she did take birth control pills for a few years. "When I got into college," she said, "I did sleep with a half-dozen boys during the first two years, before I started a real relationship, seeing one guy who was more important than anyone else. When I was eighteen, I guess I just got curious about sex, or else I was afraid I was going to miss something. That was another stage," Kit said. "But it's not something I could sit down and talk to my mother about."

Parental Anger

In the early 1970s, the *New Yorker* published a cartoon that probably could run today. The drawing showed two young women walking down a school corridor.

"My parents don't care what I do," one of them is saying, "as long as it does not come to their attention."

It is possible today for teenagers who are seventeen or younger to obtain the most sophisticated forms of birth control, with or without the attention of their parents. Many parents may not like the idea. They may not endorse it. They may be offended by it. But it is a fact of contemporary life in most communities.

Some time ago, a volunteer at a Long Island office of Planned Parenthood told this story:

A worried mother called the office, seeking a VD test for her daughter who, she discovered, had just become sexually involved with her boy friend.

"Perhaps she ought to come in for birth control counseling," the volunteer said.

"Birth control!" the mother interrupted, her voice rising

several octaves. "My daughter's only sixteen—she isn't old enough."

The parental attitude is understandable. But it also reflects the emerging pattern reported by family planners for more than a decade. More than 90 percent of the teenagers who do come into clinics for birth control counseling have been sexually active for almost a year before they seek advice.

Teenagers like Ronni, in fact, usually do not know they can seek advice from Planned Parenthood, or an adolescent clinic, or anywhere else, without the approval of their parents. Some find out when a pregnancy test is needed.

For those in the field of family planning, the issue of teen sex is, of course, a sensitive issue. As a Planned Parenthood official said: "We don't encourage teenagers to become sexually active. If they do, we encourage them to talk to their parents. But if a girl is thirteen or fourteen or fifteen, and she's sexually active, she can come in and get birth control counseling with or without her parent's consent." When challenged, Planned Parenthood has been prepared to go to court to argue on behalf of the teenager's right to privacy and her right to prevent pregnancy.

The facts of contemporary life deeply disturb parents. But the fact that thousands of teenagers are sexually active—and do not take any precautions against unwanted pregnancy—is also a disturbing fact of life.

Over the years, the tone and content of sex education in the public school have become more and more frank. But the issue of birth control will remain controversial. A majority of parents, perhaps, will continue to feel irate and abandoned when they discover that their daughters have turned to a private clinic for birth control services without their knowledge. And many vent their anger by calling the clinic.

"After we talk," a nurse in a family planning clinic recalled, "they begin to express the feeling that they have failed as parents, that they've lost control of their children, or that they have been rejected. . . . And some worry that we are promoting sexual experimentation by making birth control available—even though most girls come in long after they've started their sexual relationships."

Clinics have also reported a punitive response from some adults. This point of view is sometimes expressed: "I think kids ought to get pregnant, to teach them a lesson."

But the viewpoint is seldom expressed by parents whose children—male or female—are involved in a relationship that resulted in pregnancy.

Open debates between parents and children over sexual freedom is relatively new in this country. And it can be highly charged emotionally. At a birth control seminar in a suburban community, for example, a mother of a fourteen-year-old girl pleaded for "more talk about morals" by family planning clinics. Teenagers answered that clinics are "for birth control, not moral control." And one teenager added: "It's sad that we can't talk to our parents about sex without everybody getting angry."

Large numbers of teenagers, however, can't or won't talk to their parents about their sexual feelings and behavior, according to reports from family planning clinics. At the same time, national surveys conducted by social scientists show that at least 40 to 45 percent of all adolescents become sexually active by their late teens. And according to doctors, nurses, teachers, and young people themselves, most still refrain from using modern birth control methods.

Why?

In many states, public laws prohibit the sale of contraceptives to minors under the age of sixteen and public health facilities are generally not open to young teenagers.

Some health departments, for instance, will offer birth control services without parental consent only to those who are eighteen or older. For sixteen-year-olds and seventeen-year-olds, these public services are available only with parental consent, if the teenagers are self-supporting, if they are married, or if they already have a child.

Most typical is the policy of a public health agency in a large suburban county, which will not offer birth control counseling to teenagers under sixteen "under any circumstance."

Often, however, there is a significant loophole—and it does provide private clinics the opportunity to offer birth control counseling to teenagers without parental knowledge or consent.

In New York State, for instance, public health laws permit "treatment" if, in the view of a doctor, "an attempt to secure parental consent would increase the risk to the person's life or health."

Assisting young people to avoid risk has been a commitment made by family planning clinics across the country. Despite sex education courses and all the modern literature on sexuality, old myths live on.

At one clinic, a nurse recalled, "a sixteen-year-old thought she couldn't get pregnant until she was eighteen." Another believed it was safe if "you had sex standing up" and some still thought pregnancy could be blocked by douching with Coke-and-aspirin after intercourse.

In such cases, the nurse said, "we do urge young girls to reconsider and to delay sexual activity until they feel they are really ready."

On the clinic wall, there was a sign that read: "If you are old enough to have children, you are old enough to decide when!"

The viewpoint has enraged many parents across the country, perhaps the majority. This response, from a mother of a fifteen-year-old, probably reflects a view held by many mothers and fathers: "Perhaps my daughter is physically old enough, but I don't think she ought to be encouraged to take a chance—either on pregnancy or on the pill."

But if teenagers are, in fact, sexually active, can parents keep alive a dialogue about sexuality with their children?

Active Help

In books and in the classroom, young people can get the facts—the facts, as they say, just the facts.

For many youngsters, the facts of a sexual education are derived almost exclusively at school and in the schoolyard. But at home, like it or not, parents do play a role. Even with their silence, they shape attitudes and feelings about sexuality.

The talk between parents and children about sex may begin at varying ages. But the emotional message about sexuality, conveyed by parents, is far more important.

From the time their children are born, parents have the power to be accepting and supportive of their youngster's sexuality. And parents who are uneasy about their own sexuality will communicate this feeling to their children.

In every generation, parents tend to be more conservative than the younger generation about sexual questions. Parental attitudes may be sharply different, especially if they were shaped in homes where sex was a taboo subject.

For parents, these long-held attitudes and feelings may be difficult to change. But the attempt can be made to open a dialogue with adolescents—even when parents and children differ sharply on the topic of sexuality. Flexibility is valuable in dealing with your children, and communication may take a special effort, perhaps, on the part of parents.

For example, a parent might tell their adolescent children directly: "Talking about this is sometimes difficult and awkward for me, but it's something we need to talk about." And the door between parents and children can be propped open.

But by preaching or by refusing to recognize the reality of sexual feelings in children and adolescents, parents can put sex off-limits to family discussion. It is important to remember: setting standards in the quality of these talks begins early in childhood.

Parents can set examples in the way they accept their children's sexuality at different ages. As early as age two, for instance, mothers and fathers are often concerned with recurring incidents of masturbation. If parents are uncomfortable or if they feel the incidents are excessive, they can distract the child in deft ways—rather than slapping the child's hand or scolding or telling the child that "that's wrong" or "that's not allowed."

Such messages communicate the notion to children that there is something wrong with their genitals, that touching that part of the body is wrong, that there is something wrong with that part of the body and something wrong with sex itself.

At age five, youngsters sometimes "play doctor," exploring the bodies of children of the opposite sex, an early adventure in the mystery of sexuality. Here, too, parents can simply distract children with other choices, other games. Offering another activity to the game-players is preferable.

Parents can be firm in setting guidelines. They may be perturbed when they discover their children have been engaged in some form of "playing doctor" and they may prefer to discourage such explorations. But there is no need to communicate hysteria, as if a major disaster had occurred. There are some sound reasons, however, to support parental concern.

It is, after all, usually a secret game for most children, and they can feel uneasy and guilty in taking part in such a recognized taboo. So while their sexual curiosity is natural, the nature of the investigation might be questioned.

Instead of learning about the opposite sex from the little girl or boy next door, children can be offered the inside truth from books and pictures instead, made available by their parents. Mothers and fathers can make it clear that there are substitute sources of information that will provide answers to their children's questions.

In the pre-adolescent years, boys and girls can be prepared for natural and expected changes in their bodies. Boys can be told about masturbation and nocturnal emissions. Girls can be informed about the positive aspects of growing up—about masturbation, the menstrual cycle, and the physical changes that signal the onset of womanhood. Each can benefit by learning about changes in the opposite sex.

In some families, such conversations may seem taboo. But such avoidance interferes with the adolescent's emerging sense of sexual identity. Such interference does not keep adolescents from experimenting with sex, but it may keep them from enjoying their sexuality later.

Feeling Good

Teenagers often feel so good about their emerging sexuality that they go to extremes in showing off the latest symbols of sexuality. Wearing hip clothing, often too tight-fitting in the eyes of their parents, is one example.

How can parents handle the crisis of the tight sweater or the showdown over the overly snug jeans?

A father might say, for instance, "How pretty you look . . . how womanly you look," affirming his daughter's expression of her sexual identity. One of the goals, after all, is to affirm the rightness of sexual development, male and female. And harsh criticism of revealing clothing can interfere with this affirmation.

Understandably, many parents will find their children's choice of dress disturbing. Sweaters, jeans, or bathing suits may seem too provocative or too seductive or simply inappropriate for a particular time or place.

Parents can let their children know how they feel about their attire without appearing to criticize or to demean the sexuality of their teenagers—simply stating that they would prefer to see their children in less revealing clothing, without resorting to comments on the sexual explicitness of the attire.

Often, parents and children will reverse their positions on what is "too extreme" in style and behavior. At times, for instance, younger adolescents feel more embarrassed about revealing bathing suits and tight pairs of jeans than their parents—especially when they are with their parents. Some teenage girls may regress and feel more comfortable in floppy, figure-concealing clothing at home. At school, the same adolescents will feel quite at ease in more flattering and revealing outfits, to remain competitive with their peers.

Parents also may be upset with teenagers who seem preoccupied with nude photos and sexually graphic pictures. When parents find such sexual exhibits offensive, they have every right, of course, to express their views. But it helps to avoid a frontal attack on their children's new interest in sex. The goal is to shift the focus away from criticism of sexuality and to less personal issues involving taste and standards of propriety set within each family.

Boundary lines can be drawn, enunciating moral values and standards of esthetic taste. Parents may state firmly, for instance, that they do not wish to see sexually explicit photos on display in their living room or elsewhere in the house, outside the privacy of their teenager's own room. But the message should avoid a condemnation of adolescent sexuality or natural curiosity about sex, which might not create another sexual taboo an adolescent would be tempted to defy.

Parents may be offended by the crass merchandizing of sex and sexuality. But their actions as official censor at home could send another message: that there is something wrong with sex and something wrong in their children's interest in sex. Parents need to make the distinction between their feelings about sex and their attitudes toward sexual crudities that may find their way into the home and into the hands of curious adolescents of all ages.

The Wrong Arena

From early childhood, boys and girls learn attitudes toward sex from their parents. If the message is silent, that too is a communication.

Silence can pique curiosity and create intrigue, building another arena in which teenagers can be tempted to defy their parents. During adolescence, when young people face a special identity crisis—attempting to define themselves as sexual adults—there often comes an irresistible urge to shape that definition of identity by defying parental authority and standards.

It can be a dangerous impulse, because teenagers may hurt themselves by acting out sexually in their attempt to defy their parents. So parental restrictiveness is also dangerous and often can backfire, making sex and sexuality an even more attractive arena of defiance.

Often, sexual experimentation is lumped with drugs and alcohol in adult discussions, reflecting the extreme concern of parents that their children will hurt themselves by acting-out in these taboo areas. But by the time a child reaches adolescence, parents really cannot control their teenager's behavior, no matter how strict the rules of the home are.

When adolescents do choose to defy their parents, they are apt to question standards in the way most likely to upset and shock their family. And sex often is the most convenient arena in which to act out adolescent defiance of authority.

Parents have their limits. What they can do is communicate their wishes, feelings, and fears. Adolescents often will do what they chose to do, in any case. But parents can move to avoid problems.

For instance, if parents are concerned that their sons or daughters or their friends will drink too much, grind out cigarettes on the floors, or sneak upstairs into the master bedroom, they should not make the house available for parties when no one is home to provide an adult presence.

Parents can make it clear, repeatedly, that such behavior will not be condoned, even if you cannot prevent sexual activity elsewhere or you cannot supervise your adolescent's life at every moment.

Some parents do accept the notion that adolescents, at a certain age, will begin to explore and experiment with sex—and they view this without alarm, as a normal part of growing up. These parents can explore the possibility of birth control with their children, and they can broach the subject of possible sex-related diseases without making sex an ultimate taboo.

Often, teenagers respond with anger. Can't use the house? They'll find other places, they say. But at least they will not have parental approval unless you decide to give it, and the awareness of parental guidelines is crucial to teenagers—because sexuality is a new and uncharted sea, where there are no past boundaries and no memories to draw on.

Knowing how to act and how not to act is still a question mark at this age, but for some adolescents, the message from parents often is: "We don't want to know what you are doing." And often, this can be interpreted as a sanction for any behavior at all.

At the same time, it is also crucial for parents to refrain from denying the sexual maturity of their children. The sexual feelings of teenagers are often very strong and need to find expression in some way. Some sublimation is possible, through music, dancing, and sports. But when parents attempt to repress sexuality by denying its existence, they set the stage for trouble, anger, and resentment. And this denial can interfere with the adolescent's own concept of who he or she is.

Often this denial comes simply by refusing to recognize the adolescent's heightened awareness and interest in sex. If an adolescent boy or girl is in a dating relationship, talk is avoided about birth control, pregnancy, and other aspects of a sexual relationship.

Often, there is no communication about sex at all, at a time when adolescents might want to seek advice.

Parents may not want to provide sexual opportunities—place or time—for their children. They are not obligated to endorse their children's sexual behavior if they are uncomfortable with it. But while sexual activity may not be condoned, parents can still communicate the message that they are available—as an emotional support.

For many parents, this will be a difficult role to play. But the existence of heightened sexual interest should not be denied. And when an adolescent is committed to a sexual relationship, parents need to be in a position to listen. Adolescents can easily feel abandoned, especially when they know they are acting in a way that will evoke parental disapproval.

So at crucial times, parents can pass on the message: "We may not think what you're doing is a good idea—but you still can come to us. We are still here for you."

Who's in Charge

You are.

As parents, you still can provide firm and consistent expectations—even though your children may challenge the limits you set—rebelling simply to test your resolve and define themselves.

Your power to set limits—curfews on weekends, party rules, school night behavior—is still important. Parents continue to be surprised, even shocked, when they discover that their children have had sexual experiences even when, in retrospect, all the signs of sexual interest and activity were there.

Many parents hold on to the belief that their child is the one that isn't involved with sex—despite recurring surveys and statistics that testify that large numbers of boys and girls will be sexually active by the time they complete high school or enter college.

Adolescents, of course, are confronted with conflicting standards of sexual behavior every day. The standards most widely professed by traditional parents are constantly and visibly challenged in movies, on TV, in magazine ads, on news broadcasts, and by the behavior of the older generation itself.

The message from parents is: Abstain!

But all around them, teenagers hear the other side of the story—and it is much more enticing. For parents and their children, communication is a crucial goal—and these social contradictions also need to be faced, once again, by confronting realities rather than pretending they do not exist.

ABUSING DRUGS

For parents in this country, the use of drugs by their children is a frightening nightmare. It brings little comfort to know that the great majority of teenagers are not drug abusers—even those who have succumbed to peer pressure or curiosity and experimented on occasion.

The mother of a seventeen-year-old boy at Choate remarked: "I know that he's serious about his future and a responsible kid—but when the drug bust at the school made headlines, I was relieved he wasn't one of them." She even asked her son's girl friend, "Please tell me if he ever has any problems about drugs."

Teenage use of drugs has been a major concern among parents since the mid-1960s, when the use of marijuana, and later, LSD and harder drugs, began to spread from the subculture of adult urban life into the suburban high schools.

During the 1950s, students rarely overdosed on six-packs of beer, even though intense concern about drinking was expressed in the years after World War II. But once again, community leaders have raised the issue, sounding a new alarm over teen drinking and driving. But the problem of alcohol abuse by teenagers is far from new and has been perceived as a community concern for decades, only overshadowed by public preoccupation with drug abuse in high schools and colleges during the late 1960s.

Now we are seeing drug abuse among many younger adolescents, under the age of fifteen. When these problems emerge, they also serve as clear-cut evidence of long-buried emotional disturbance. Like other crises of childhood, they are often related to separation and loss, repressed pain, and unrecognized sadness.

Drug use may be especially infuriating to parents because many drugs tend to anesthetize—and their children's conduct may become casual, cavalier, unresponsive and downright irksome. If parents can stay calm and try to look beneath the surface behavior, they can aid their children before serious harm is done. Despite the allure of cocaine, the current drug of choice among the stars, the great pain-killers of our culture— alcohol and marijuana—are still the two most popular drugs among young users and abusers.

In the following pages, we look at Sid's experience and his slide into the drug culture at age thirteen. We also examine the stunning increase of smoking among adolescent girls since the early 1970s, just when adults started to cut down on the cigarette habit.

For parents, drug use—including nicotine—is a perplexing problem. The roots of the problem, found often in children's unexpressed anger and anxiety, are even more alarming. But children can be helped, even during their most defiant and petulant years.

Sid: In a new town

Sid was fourteen when the police brought him to the hospital on a Halloween night.

"We found him on the beach," a police officer told Sid's father. "He was high as a kite, running along the beach, yelling his head off, swinging a bat."

Sid thought that he was being pursued by a monster in the form of a yellow ball of fire. The fantasy was a bizarre variation on the costumed kids he had seen along the beach, celebrating the holiday. "Kill it, kill it," Sid was screaming.

Two friends brought him back to his father's beach house on Fire Island. Sid, whose parents were divorced, had been visiting his father during a fall break at school. At his father's house, his frenetic monologue continued. His father and stepmother were terrified, unaware of what was happening. In this isolated community, there was no doctor.

But they called their doctor on shore, who urged them to get Sid to a hospital as soon as possible. Perhaps it was something Sid had eaten, the doctor speculated. It was: a handful of peyote buttons.

Sid's father called a friend with a boat, who took Sid across Great South Bay to a landing where an ambulance was waiting. In the emergency room of a local hospital, the doctors spotted the problem without delay: a hallucinogenic drug.

Later, under sedation after the hallucinations ebbed, Sid told them about the peyote. "This kid needs psychiatric help," one of the interns said. But Sid's father was too upset to act, too embarrassed by his son's behavior and by his own sense of failure. So Sid's story did not emerge until years later, in therapy sessions, when he was in college.

Sid recalled that he began using drugs when he was thirteen and some of the events of his Halloween evening in the emergency room remained in his memory. It was a nightmarish trip. Finally the hallucinations subsided.

Lying on a cot in the emergency room, he was exhausted. His father was there in the room. Sid felt confused. He recognized his father and his new stepmother, but he was still not sure who he was. Suddenly he was overcome by a wave of terror. He had never felt so afraid. But his father, overcome by his own feelings of despair, had no room to take in of his son's feelings. Sid recalled that there was just silence in the room.

Early Losses

It was not the first time that Sid had felt alone. Just before his thirteenth birthday, he experienced a severe trauma. Without warning, Sid's parents split up. Sid's mother moved to a small town in the Midwest, and soon after, she remarried. The relocation came at a time when Sid was happy in school, doing

B-plus work in his eighth grade class. After some adjustment problems in earlier grades, he was secure within his small circle of school friends.

Sid knew very little about his parents' decision to divorce or why it happened. It was quite abrupt, shrouded in mystery for Sid. It simply happened. So it was early November when he and his mother moved to a new town. Suddenly Sid was in a new house in another state, in a community he had never visited, where he had no friends or relatives. For Sid, an only child, that year's Thanksgiving dinner came and went with no sense of festivity. At the time, Sid was going through another vulnerable period, just entering puberty. He was feeling more alone than ever.

Remembrance of Pain Past

Sid's sense of crisis might have been eased. He was suddenly transplanted into a new and foreign scene, but a number of steps could have been taken to ease the adjustment to unwanted realities:

- Sid's parents, for instance, might have talked about their breakup and the move to a new town, to set the emotional stage for Sid before it happened.

- A visit to the new community and Sid's new school might have lowered his feelings of apprehension.

- The move might have been timed to coincide with the new school year, to soften Sid's feelings of loss.

- And Sid might have been encouraged to express his feelings of sadness, anger, and pain.

The divorce was a matter of reality. For Sid and his parents, it was hard to adjust to the new situation. For everyone, the new living arrangements brought a difficult period of change. But it was not the end of the world.

Sid thought it was.

He sat in a strange new classroom, filled with children he did not know and did not want to know. Nothing looked or felt or even smelled familiar. He missed his old and trusted friends, his boyhood room, the streets of his old neighborhood. He felt very sorry for himself.

The feelings were quite appropriate, but Sid kept them to himself. Once, when he was moping around the house, his mother tried to cheer him up, by reminding him that, after all, he had his own room in a new and modern house, "much more than many children were privileged to have." So Sid kept his mouth shut.

Empathy from his parents might have eased Sid's pain. Sometimes, as adults, parents forget the pain they too experienced as children—especially if they grew up in families where the expression of sad or angry feelings was not encouraged or permitted.

But many adults have faced unsettling changes when they were growing up. Even moving across town to a new neighborhood can be jarring. Moving into a new bedroom with a different view, with different trees outside, with different houses across the street, can stir feelings of loneliness. For some children, even changing chairs at the dining room table can be upsetting: a loss of something familiar in a child's garden of possible terrors.

So Sid was angry and sad and hurt. But his needs were not acknowledged by his parents, since he never voiced his feelings. Children often have feelings that are very different from those of adults. And even if parents once endured similar pain, they sometimes bury those feelings—making it difficult for them to give their children empathy and support.

They may recall teenage upheavals but they may not remember the feelings, because they were not fully experienced or they were unexpressed at the time. If parents were able to recapture vividly the feelings of their own childhood traumas, they would be more likely to understand and to accept their children's anger and sadness.

The Parental Wars

Sid began to experiment with drugs a few months after he arrived in his new community.

He had felt that the children in his new school were "very different." It was not an unreasonable feeling. The move to a new community had come at a time when his own sense of adolescent identity was fragile.

And the children in his new school probably were different. Arriving in the midst of the academic year, Sid was confronted by social cliques designed to exclude newcomers and intruders. The message was an old and clear one: There was no place for Sid.

Once again, it was another reality.

Sid's mother had no power to change schoolyard politics or to intervene in the mechanics of neighborhood alliances. But Sid might have been encouraged to talk about his feelings of isolation and disappointment. However, at this crucial time, Sid's father was unavailable, and Sid hardly knew his new stepfather. His mother was working full-time at a new job. So it seemed to Sid that he had lost his mother and his father and all of his old friends.

What he found was a new shelter in this storm—a group of young adolescents at school who were also outsiders, troubled and lonely, and into the drug scene.

Many of them seemed familiar to him. They were outcasts and they took him in. He could talk to them. The kinship was there almost from the start. His parents felt that something was wrong with Sid, but with these new friends, he was accepted, without question and without criticism.

The crucial factor, of course, was not friendship. It was drugs—and drugs really did help.

For the first time in a long time, Sid felt less pain. With his new friends, he smoked grass for the first time. Then he began to use uppers and downers. "After that, it was whatever was around." He began to feel he was part of the group.

He had just turned fourteen when he met his new friends. Through the spring and summer, he was stoned most of the time. In the fall, when he began high school, his grades began to drop for the first time since fifth grade.

For Sid, the first report card brought some results he longed for more than anything else: His mother started to pay attention to him. It was not the kind of attention he wanted, not affectionate at all, but it was better than nothing.

There were many fights. Sid would return home during dinner or after the evening meal was over. Sometimes he would stagger in at 8 or 9 o'clock. His mother and stepfather were furious.

"Where were you?"

"What were you doing?"

"What's wrong with you?"

Sid mumbled answers, shrugged off threats, ignored punishment. During these exchanges with his parents, he wished that he could disappear or be invisible. He hated being home. And when he was with his friends, his use of drugs escalated.

On some weekend evenings, he would come home very late, having forgotten his key. When he awakened his mother and stepfather, he could not understand why they were so angry. "Big deal . . . They could go back to sleep," he thought.

On other nights, he was almost too stoned to make it to the front door. His parents continued their warnings and criticisms, and once, his mother told him: "One more time and you live somewhere else." She had made that threat before.

During this confrontation, the angriest in the family's history, Sid nearly nodded out.

Feelings of Failure

Parents cannot prepare their children for all the traumas of adolescence. But as a crisis surfaces, parents can listen with care. They can make an effort to understand their children's deeper feelings and needs.

Sid's mother and father both resisted the idea of professional counseling. Such a suggestion intensified their own feelings of incompetence. In their minds, it would have constituted an admission that they had failed as parents. Feeling guilty themselves, they diligently whipped themselves with those feelings.

At such times, parents should not be too harsh on themselves. Not even if, inadvertently, they have inflicted pain on their children. Often, they too were victims as children—something they need to remember in their dealings with their own offspring. As mothers and fathers, they often discover one of the roots to a problem in parenting: the desire to idealize their own childhood. When parents do blot out the reality of their past, they are less likely to remember their own childhood pain—and they are more likely to inflict the same pain on their children. It is a painful truth.

But if parents can recognize that they might be doing to their own children what once was done to them—if they can accept that possibility—then they can begin to open a door, to strengthen their children—and when it is necessary, to seek professional advice without guilt. If parents do not take their own wounds seriously, it is unlikely that they can truly feel the pain of their children.

Again, empathy plays a crucial role.

The sequence is a common one. Sid was confronted with what he saw as a wall of isolation and rejection. He was on the threshold of puberty, and hormonal changes made it even more difficult for Sid to repress his intense feelings. Until then, his parents had managed to control him, to train him to be "a good boy." So he would contain or disguise his pain and anger and sadness.

Then came this biological explosion. Sid no longer could repress these feelings. He was beset with a jumble of emotions: rage and anger, sexual desire and enthusiasm, sadness and joy—a panoramic landscape of feelings. They demanded expression and denied containment. For Sid, drugs provided a new way to cap his feelings. But his parents had no idea that their son had stumbled onto this temporarily effective and dangerous means of self-medication.

Many parents have a storybook notion that, by nature, adolescents are supposed to be sullen and withdrawn. But for many youngsters in crisis, it is actually harder for them to repress feelings during this adolescent period. When Sid withdrew—suddenly becoming the family's emotional dropout—it was a signal that he was erecting new defenses against his intense feelings of rage and sadness—or at least trying to.

Those defenses became harder and harder to maintain through the turmoil of growth, the *sturm und drang* of adolescent change. When he turned to drugs, his pain was masked for a time.

Turmoil would have been a more optimistic sign.

In the real world, when confronted with visible signs of adolescent turmoil, parents might cheer—silently—from the domestic sidelines. For if there is no turmoil, there might be more to worry about.

So Sid's parents discovered. And their reaction, after all, was natural. Parents often are afraid that their child will lose control completely, so they are tempted to encourage repression.

"Grow up" is one of the stifling commands that children hear. There are others. Parents have an impulse to want a neat and tidy world for their children. And often, it is painful for parents to deal with their own forgotten feelings. When children express rage, mothers and fathers may feel they have failed because they want their child to be a reflection of "good parenting" and to be happy, perhaps as happy as they never were. Often, parents see a part of themselves in an unhappy child. But the pain or unhappiness might be a forgotten part of their own childhood. It is easy to lose contact with those early feelings.

So Sid's rage and sadness was capped at a crucial time. The Halloween crisis came after a long summer of heavy drug use. For Sid, the bad trip was a horrendous scare—and it was the last time he plotted an emotional escape with hallucinogens.

Although his parents were unable to accept the advice that their son needed counseling, Sid's drug use actually diminished in the next three years, although he did continue to smoke marijuana throughout his high school years.

It did serve a purpose—to contain his subterranean rage until he finished school. His grades were above average, although they were below his full potential. And when he was eighteen, he was accepted by a state university far from home. Qualifying for scholarship money, Sid moved away from his mother's house and cut himself off from both parents for a full year.

He supported himself with a full-time job and attended

classes at night. He did not write or call home, left no forwarding address, and pretended that his parents did not exist. It was a period of great suffering, and although Sid was economically independent, he felt terribly persecuted by his parents through the year.

In college, he emerged as a very bright young man, and he compensated for emotional problems with academic intensity, achieving high grades. But in his senior year, he ran into new trouble, confronted by the breakup of a romantic relationship. This crisis prompted him finally to seek professional counseling, and while in therapy, Sid went on to graduate school, continuing to achieve.

While in college, Sid had joined a therapy group, and in one of the sessions, the subject of loss came up. Sid related to the experience instantly:

A young women in the group recalled a childhood incident, the day her pet dog died. Her parents, she said, had been very reassuring.

"They did not pretend the dog hadn't died, so it was very painful. But they didn't tell me not to worry. Or that my dog had gone to heaven or anything like that," she recalled. "They just stayed with me. I cried and cried but I learned I could bear it."

For Sid, crying never was a viable option. Instead, in a crisis, Sid learned to shut down emotionally. And when he reached adolescence, life became so painful that shutting down became more and more difficult. Then the drug scene came along and, for a time, it was Sid's solution of choice for turning off all the painful feelings.

Chris: Puffing away

Wait now. Just a moment now. The smoke is lifting and— there she is:

Baby face with cigarette

Taking deep meaningful Clark Gable-movieland-machismo puffs

"How old do you think I am?" puffs
"Don't tell my mother" puffs
"You've come a long way baby" puffs
And look at you now . . . still baby-faced.

Chris was just a baby-faced teenager, leaning against a pillar in a shopping mall, watching the crowd go by. Hanging out.

Behind a puff of blue smoke, she steadied her Winston with moist lips. An old pro. Chris was fourteen, she said, and she had been smoking a pack and a half a day since she was twelve.

Her pal Nan, who was also fourteen and in ninth grade, said she had been a regular smoker since she was in sixth grade. She was up to a pack a day now, but no, it didn't bother her. "Only when I run," she said.

Everybody smokes, Nan said. Almost everybody in her junior high school. Sure, it's stupid. But it just gets to be a habit. She shrugged. It wasn't so bad—as long as her mother didn't find out. She always carried a breath spray to use before going home for dinner.

How did it begin?

Chris was "taught" by her older brother, who dared her to smoke a cigarette one afternoon. Nan just picked it up from her relatives. They both thought it was a pretty cool idea at first. Now? "Oh, we're just used to it," said Nan.

They had learned a lot about smoking.

Like smoking in the bathroom is a good way to get caught. Smoking on the way to school and back was the safer. Or in the shopping center, the local teen hangout in the afternoon. Only half the boys in Nan's ninth-grade class smoked, she guessed, but most of the girls did . . . about three out of four.

Why did she smoke?

"Makes you less tense," said the baby-face behind the cigarette. "At a party I can smoke like a pack and a half, all in one night. When I'm around my friends, I'm always dying for a cigarette. Or when I'm feeling bad or I'm meeting new people. Then I smoke a lot. A cigarette is like company, even when it's not lit. It gives you something to do."

Chris thought it made her look older. Tougher too. But she's not really sure why she smoked. Maybe because she wasn't allowed to. "But it would be crazy to smoke for the rest of your life," said Nan. Chris nodded. "Could you spare a cigarette?" she asked.

Chris and Nan were not really aware they are part of a national phenomenon. Something new was happening, but they were only vaguely conscious of it. At a time when millions of American adults have given up cigarette smoking—more than 30 million according to the federal record-keepers—the number of girls and young women between the ages of twelve and eighteen who smoke has almost doubled. Young females have just about caught up to their male counterparts in making smoking an equal-opportunity vice.

The turn of events has puzzled everyone, from social scientists to government researchers, from feminist theorists to lobbyists for the tobacco industry. By the late 1970s, there was even greater alarm about younger teenagers when a government survey showed that a greater percentage of twelve- to fourteen-year-old girls were smoking compared to boys the same ages. And girls from fifteen to sixteen also outsmoked their male counterparts.

But why?

Why, after all these years of terrifying school hall lectures on the danger of tobacco? Why, after all the direct and subliminal messages on the hazards of cigarettes to one's health? Why, during a time when a majority of parents eagerly informed pollsters that they would urge their children not to start the smoking habit? And why during a dramatic period when the number of adult smokers was on the decline?

Even finding a place to smoke in public has become more difficult by the mid-1980s. So answers are difficult. There is, after all, no explanation of why some young people are not tempted to smoke at all. But some teenage puffers have their own theories.

They talk of "feeling older" or "being more attractive," looking independent or "having that tough look," when they first start to smoke. But then, why don't all teenagers need a drag to relax them, to bolster their confidence, or to provide a hint of impending adulthood?

A government health official speculated that the change in teen smoking patterns might be related to the phenomenon of unisex fads and fashions. The feminist movement probably has played a role, simply because females of all ages are seeking access to all practices and provinces once open only to males.

Certainly more adult women smoke today. Women are more free and assertive in every way—and smoking may be a way of expressing a sense of freedom once associated with masculinity. Young women are more upwardly mobile and often feel the tensions of the workaday world in jobs that once were exclusively "man's work." And these young women—independent and free-wheeling—offer a powerful and attractive role model for a new generation of young girls in their early teens.

So smoking too has been "liberated," emerging as a symbol of new freedoms and greater choices. "We no longer look upon the woman who smokes as a shady character," a government health researcher observed. Young women are unlikely even to know that smoking on the street was considered a social taboo—a sure sign of poor breeding—not so many years ago. But the price of equality is often dear. In the case of smokers, the price may be a greater incidence of lung cancer.

Feminists have speculated that young women and teenage girls turn to cigarettes because of added pressure on the female in today's changing world—a world in which choices suddenly seem abundant. Possibly parents today tend to be less restrictive with their daughters. Or perhaps more young girls look upon smoking as an early outlet for defiance, even as the smoking habit itself is no longer viewed as "unacceptable" for women. Social scientists observe that the statistics about smoking simply may be moving toward equalization, "as boys and girls are treated with greater equality." There is no end to the speculation.

Tobacco industry officials too have voiced some concern. "I hope young people are aware that smoking is a controversial issue. I hope they look into the literature and decide for themselves," an official of the Tobacco Institute said some years ago.

Certainly parents have an even greater stake in introducing to their children the subject of smoking as a potential hazard to their health and their lives.

But how can parents approach the topic without their teenagers and pre-teenagers dropping a curtain of silence on the topic?

"It's just one more thing we're not suppose to do," was the way baby-faced Chris put it. But parents certainly can encourage their children to talk about it. The more they can verbalize their anxieties, the less those feelings are likely to go up in smoke, literally.

Smoking, of course, is linked to other pleasures. Peer-group pressure is a factor: Lighting up together is such an easy way to strike an adult pose prematurely. And when parents condemn smoking, another arena of potential defiance may be established, an inviting field of combat when teenagers seek to define their identities.

But in dealing with possibly harmful behavior—as in dealing with sexual acting out—parents need to make it clear that they do not condone hazardous behavior. And of course, they need to remember: If they expect their children to refrain from popular outlets for tension, such as smoking cigarettes, being a good role model themselves can sometimes—though not always—help to clear the air.

TROUBLE AT THE DINNER TABLE

When young children refuse to eat, life at home can become open warfare.

When adolescents refuse to eat, their lives usually become secretive—and their behavior can become deadly.

But dinner table combat may have been in the mobilization stage for years. Drawing on early experiences, children may feel the desire to eat when they feel lonely and yearn for emotional nourishment. Then problems with weight and body image can become a self-destuctive force in adolescence and adulthood.

For Jane, not eating became the passion of her life. Her behavior, a secret until it was almost too late, was rooted in her early relationship with her parents and in her desperate need to feel in control of her body and her own life—even if she risked losing it.

The road back from anorexia is uncertain. It is a very destructive disorder, and its victims often require lengthy psychotherapy. The support of the family during this period, of course, is crucial. But it can be an extremely difficult time for the parents as well as the victim. Often, the illness is life-threatening, with setbacks recurring often and recovery slow. The utmost patience is demanded of those who care.

Jane: Fighting anorexia

At sixteen, most of Jane's girl friends envied her: She was a bright teenager, envied by her friends for her fresh good looks and her academic success at school.

But Jane was troubled. Two years before, when she was just starting high school, she had been rejected by her first boy friend. He was a junior named Tom, one of the stars of the varsity swimming team. They went out together for a month or so during the summer. Then, when classes began, he decided Jane was too young for him.

Jane was very hurt. But it had been a difficult summer anyway. That July, Jane bought a bikini for the first time. Although she was slim and athletic, she was acutely self-conscious and modest about her maturing body. Years before, her father had joked affectionately about her little-girl chubbiness. But as an adolescent, Jane fretted about her father's comments.

"Fat . . . too fat," she'd say, examining her legs as if they had been placed on the wrong torso, a mean trick, she thought. Her preoccupation became a familiar litany at the dinner table. At first, her parents found it boring. Later, they were annoyed.

"All you think about is yourself," Jane's father said.

His criticism was accurate. But his observations did nothing to ease Jane's anxiety. Self-consciousness is predictable, after all, during this period of adolescent change, something parents might anticipate. But when Jane was criticized or ridiculed, she felt silenced.

Hating Everyone

In high school, Jane became even more obsessed with fatness. Specifically, she was overwhelmed with a fear of gaining weight.

What was fatness?

Anyone who watched TV or read junk magazines knew what fatness meant. It meant being rejected by boys. It meant being laughed at by girls. It meant being alone and out of control.

Jane's behavior worked against her. She was very critical of everyone around her. High school wasn't turning out the way it was supposed to. She disliked her teachers and the stupid boys in her class and the girls who talked about clothes all the time.

But most of all, Jane hated fatness. And a new pattern of behavior emerged. Jane stopped eating.

It began in the spring of her freshman year. Her mother had just taken a part-time job and Jane missed talking to her in the late afternoons. Now summer was coming, and Jane weighed five pounds more than she had the previous summer. Of course, she was an inch taller, but that did not matter. At first, her parents were unaware of the anorexic pattern. It emerged slowly:

- Jane began to exercise with a passion. Playing junior varsity basketball, she outran everyone.

- She skipped meals, always with well-planned excuses. She never wanted to upset her family.

- While she told her parents she was having dinner at a friend's house, she would tell her host that she had eaten earlier.

- Losing weight, she wore loose-fitting clothes to disguise her thinness, knowing that her mother would be alarmed if she learned how much weight Jane had lost since early spring.

- Often she would take her dinner to her room—to do homework, she said. Or she would ask permission to watch a TV program during dinner. It gave Jane a chance to dispose of a large portion of food down the toilet.

During this period, Jane grew withdrawn and depressed. Her grades began to slip. Despite all her frenetic activity at school, she felt she was the only person left in the world, a survivor of some universal catastrophe.

Jane never became involved with the drug crowd in school. She seemed to be a stable, goal-oriented, highly motivated young woman. But one afternoon, on a shopping street, she met Tom, her old boy friend, who was starting college. In a moment of tightly reined hysteria, Jane told him she was feeling "so turned off" that she was planning to swallow a whole bottle of pills. Upset by Jane's outburst, Tom called her mother. And Jane's emotional health became an official family issue for the first time.

Jane wasn't really planning to swallow a handful of pills. She was just trying to see if Tom cared for her at all. But yes, she admitted later, sometimes she really did feel like disappearing.

Her parents were frightened but were unsure what to do. By now, they were aware how painfully thin Jane had become. And when Jane permitted them to discover the full details of her anorexic behavior, her parents were horrified by both her weight loss and her bizarre behavior. After a consultation with a psychologist at school, Jane entered therapy.

Many of the early sessions dealt with Jane's feeling of rejection during the previous summer. The unhappy romance with a seventeen-year-old boy, however, was only a signpost on the crisis road. In therapy, Jane's relationship with her family soon became the focal point. The breakup with Tom, her first boy friend, painful in itself, had stirred deeper feelings of rejection, dealing with her father.

Jane had felt hurt for a long time. Nothing she did or said made her father happy. It seemed that she could never please him, even when she was little. She remembered the way he talked to her when she was six or seven. She was a little chubby then. First he would tell her how pretty she was. Then, when Jane's mother gave her a second helping of cake or ice cream, he would say, "Now what kind of a diet is that?"

Jane's life seemed to be filled with double messages. Her father was proud of her schoolwork, but whenever she did well, he'd suggest how much better she could do. Jane never showed her hurt feelings. But in therapy, Jane made a startling discovery: that one of her most crucial childhood needs—to be perfect—was connected to her anorexic pattern.

The pattern was a familiar one: Jane felt out of control, and much of her behavior was designed to give her the feeling of regained control. So while she never lost her desire to eat, she forced herself to hold in these urges. She could avoid eating even when she was desperately hungry.

There were sexual connotations as well. Jane's behavior depressed any sexual feelings that might have surfaced during this adolescent period.

By not eating, Jane felt that she was keeping her body small and child-like. And without understanding the process, she was postponing any recognition of herself as an adult and a sexual being. In this way, she felt she had to become the master of her body and all its appetites.

The Gains in Losing

Jane's behavior actually fulfilled a number of her goals:

1. It gave her a feeling of total control over her body.

2. It allowed her to delay adulthood and what growing up meant to her: sexuality and separation from her family. By starving herself, for instance, she stopped her menstrual periods completely.

3. It prompted her mother to quit her part-time afternoon job so that she could be there when Jane came home after school.

4. And, like an act of suicide, it gave Jane a way to punish both her parents for criticizing her and controlling her.

During this period, sex was not a conscious issue for Jane. In fact, she had become, quite suddenly, a bit of a prude. In talks with her girl friends, she insisted that boys and girls should be virgins when they married. Her friends thought she was "weird," Jane recalled later.

One weekend, she was horrified that a brother of one of her friends brought his college girl friend home for a weekend. Jane felt betrayed. She had always looked up to the boy, like an older brother. He was always so nice to her. "Not that kind of boy," Jane said to herself. Later, she admitted she was jealous and hurt—just the way she felt when Tom told her she was too young. Jane was not conscious of her feelings about her friend's brother. So when he came home with his girlfriend, she simply was flooded with shapeless anxieties. Although her focus was on the taboo of premarital sex, her negative reaction to sex was rooted in her fear the loss of control that sex represented.

Jane's reaction was not unusual. During adolescence, when teenagers are so troubled with problems of identity and separation, some do protect themselves with a religiosity that can be frightening to parents. While Jane did not join a cult movement, she did embrace a moral code that was—for the time being—far more strict than her peers held. It was, perhaps, another signal that she was not ready to leave the safe world of childhood.

After a year in therapy, Jane still did not believe that she was an attractive person. She was still afraid that boys would like her only if she was perfect. And what did being perfect mean?

The question made Jane hesitate. Having a good figure and a dazzling smile, she said. But that was silly, she admitted. She was much more than that, wasn't she? More than just a surface image? Of course. She understood that intellectually. But emotionally, Jane was not convinced.

Still, she became more aware that her need to be seen as perfect by everyone was irrational, unnecessary, and probably impossible.

So she took a long step toward confronting her lifelong feeling of inadequacy.

Understanding the Anorexic Teenager

Jane's profile is a familiar one:

The anorexic is usually female, overdependent and compliant.

She feels a need to be outstanding and to please her parents.

She does not answer back when criticized.

She seldom seems angry.

She claims she has few complaints about her family, and
she rarely asserts herself.

There are other signs too. The anorexic is usually out of
touch with her own body and what it needs. She can avoid
signals of hunger and fatigue with ease. Jane, for instance,
excelled in sports but tended to overexert herself. Once, when
she had just begun to play basketball, early in the season, her
level of play was so excessive that one of her coaches warned
her she might hurt herself.

Even though she appeared to be independent, stubborn,
even defiant, much of Jane's behavior was a mask of bravado.
It helped to cover up her feelings of low self-esteem and powerlessness and her vulnerability to criticism, especially from her
father.

Before the onset of anorexic behavior, parents might look
for some of the surprising early warning signs.

Often, teenagers such as Jane present a clear profile of the
perfectionist: superconformist, often high-achieving, dependent, parent-pleasing. Often, such children have never been
treated as "separate" individuals, since their parents often
have difficulty seeing them as independent personalities.

- Their polite behavior is praised and encouraged.

- Their suppression of anger is applauded.

- Their achievements, scholastic and athletic, are given
  high priority.

Parents may see such children as the enhancement of their
own lives—satisfying their own needs and fulfilling their
dreams. So the "personhood" of their children may not be
acknowledged.

Often, in therapy sessions, there is a sense that the members of such families are enmeshed. Often, they will speak for
each other. And when one is asked a question, another will

answer, as if each knew what other members of the family were thinking.

In Jane's case, she was most dependent on her mother and was upset when her mother returned to work, stirring old fears of separation.

Often, in such cases, there are earlier separation problems when children begin school and leave home for the first time. Jane later recalled that she insisted her mother sit in the back of her class for almost a week when she began kindergarten.

In therapy, it became clear that Jane found it hard to make a distinction between what she really wanted and what her parents wanted for her. She admitted to herself that she had tried out for the school basketball team because of her parents' pressure to try out for a varsity sport.

She was, after all, so talented, they said. But at the time, Jane had felt a great sense of conflict, because she felt she had too many exams in the offing, and there were also other activities she was more interested in.

She felt she had no identity of her own and could not make her own decisions. So she did what her parents wanted. Doing exactly what her parents demanded, after all, was expected from "the perfect child," even a chubby one.

She became more and more compliant; at the same time her parents grew more controlling.

Then came the onset of Jane's anorexic pattern:

1. She began to focus intensely on her body.

2. She changed her eating pattern, not giving in to hunger or fatigue.

3. She felt a secret source of pride in refusing to give in to her physical needs.

4. If any sexual desires had existed, they disappeared with the onset of Jane's anorexic symptoms. The emergence of strong sexual desires during adolescence is an unfamiliar event and, understandably, even more disturbing to an adolescent who feels an excessive need to remain in control at all times—to please her parents. Receiving either direct or indirect messages that sex was taboo, Jane elimi-

nated the problem by reining in both hunger and sexuality at the same time. As a result of her anorexic behavior, Jane suffered a wide range of problems.

- She became more isolated from her friends.

- Concentrating in school became more difficult.

- Her menstrual period ceased, and her girl friends signalled to her that something was "wrong" with her.

- And as time passed, she moved toward a physical disaster.

In Jane's case, perhaps her parents might have been more supportive if they had known how easily Jane was wounded by criticism. They might have sensed possible problems in her overly compliant nature and her intense urge to overachieve. But in such cases, mothers and fathers should not feel they are the "cause" of complex problems such as anorexic behavior. A number of facts, however, are important to recognize:

1. In dealing with anorexia, professional assistance is crucial, in the form of therapy as well as appropriate medical attention.

2. Recovery is usually slow, and setbacks are frequent.

3. A therapist should be selected who has knowledge of the illness and an ability to develop a sense of trust with a young person.

With the support of parents and professional help, this crisis can be confronted.

ACCIDENTAL LIVING

The fracture may be a lucky break.

For many children, mishaps such as a fall from a bike, a collision in a gym, walking into a door, can serve as early warnings of other problems, hidden from both parent and child. "Accident-prone" children will show their parents, if they are paying attention, that their "accidents" are not accidents at all. It is wise to be on the alert for these patterns. They are signals of emotional trouble.

Children are not aware of their self-destructive ways of coping with their feelings. These feelings are most often associated with important events in a child's life—events that arouse emotions that for some reason were unexpressed. Often children will feel angry, for example, when they feel abandoned by a parent.

An angry child will often wish that the parent would die or be hurt in some way. This causes the child to feel that he or she is "bad." This guilt can be eased by the self-inflicted "accident."

Children often feel they have been abandoned by a parent even when they are the ones to leave—as in Fred's case. In addition, for both Fred and Sara, there were benefits—such as getting attention and affection. For children who feel deprived of such emotional nurturing, accidents often bring these rewards.

Parents might encourage these children to express their feelings whenever there is a change in their lives, especially one involving separation and loss. Often a child needs to be told that it is all right to feel so angry and even to wish someone dead. Thoughts and feelings are always permissible. Fred and Sara did not think so.

For Sara, who was twelve, deep-rooted problems might have been deadly. In the case of Fred, who was seventeen, his freshman year in college began with a series of disasters.

Sara: When a father leaves

One Sunday morning, Sara took a large carving knife from a kitchen drawer and locked herself in the upstairs bathroom.

This shocking turn of events came in the midst of a family squabble that had suddenly escalated into a frightening scene. It began with a pair of jeans. They were too tight, said Lily, Sara's mother. They were not at all appropriate for a Mother's Day visit to Sara's grandmother.

"Why not?" Sara asked.

"Because I said so," her mother said.

It was a familiar match between a maturing twelve-year-old and her mother: an opening service and then an intensifying volley of threats and accusations. The point usually ended in glum silence.

"Well," said Sara, "you can go to Grandma's yourself."

That was just like Sara, her mother replied. She never thought about anyone else's feelings, never helped with the household chores, the way her eight-year-old sister Karen did.

"And look at the way you dress," Sara's mother screamed. "You would never act this way if your father were here."

Sara, in tears now, rushed into the kitchen, grabbed a knife and ran up the stairs. "If you don't leave me alone, I'll kill myself," she shouted. There was a flat quality in Sara's voice that fightened her mother.

After a moment of hesitation, Lily went to the phone. The first call she made was to her therapist.

"Sara's locked herself in the bathroom with a knife," she said.

"Well, talk to her," her therapist said. "And perhaps you should call the police."

Sara listened to her mother's phone conversation from the bathroom, staring out the window at the old family car in the driveway. She was just six years old when they had bought it. Her sister Karen was two. When she looked at the car, she missed her father.

Sara's father, Arthur, had been living in another city since December. That winter, he and Lily had decided to separate. Twice a month, Sara would see her father at his new house or he would return for a weekend visit. But it was hardly like having him home.

The upheaval began a few weeks after Thanksgiving. About a month later, Sara's father and mother told the children they were separating and that their father would be in another community.

Sara remembered her father's first visit in January. She was so happy to see him. When he arrived at noon on a Sunday, she raced down the stairs at full speed. Tripping on the carpet, she fell on the landing. At first she thought she had broken her ankle, but it turned out to be just a bad sprain.

Her father picked her up and carried her to the car. Then he drove her to the hospital emergency room and waited while the doctor strapped her ankle. Despite the pain, it felt good to have him back again.

Sara looked at the big carving knife resting on the sink. She picked it up and traced a thin line across her left wrist, about an inch and a half long.

It was just a nick. And when Sara saw the blood, she was startled. She put the knife back on the sink. Outside, Lily had been pounding on the door. She was frantic. Sara covered her wrist with toilet paper and opened the bathroom door.

Talking It Out

Sara agreed to talk to a counselor the following week. On the first visit, her mother came along and talked to the therapist privately.

Lily was bewildered. In the past few months, Sara seemed dramatically changed. She was impossible to get along with. Just a year before, she was such a good girl, her mother said. Now no one in the house could do anything right, as far as Sara was concerned. She claimed that she hated her sister, Karen, and she never mentioned her father. It seemed as if Sara barely noticed that he had moved out of the house, she told the counselor.

Sara's mother felt helpless. Suddenly, Sara was always angry, talked back to her, neglected household chores, even stayed out late at night, although Lily was sure Sara wasn't involved with any boys.

Sara's mother conceded that she too was not in the best of moods. She missed the daily support of her husband and felt she was juggling too many lives. But she had just started to date a new man, and a serious relationship seemed possible. She was also seeing a therapist, and she felt she was beginning to rebuild her own life. So when her therapist had suggested that Sara might benefit from counseling, her mother immediately agreed.

In her first counseling sessions, Sara did not mention her father at all. She appeared to be indifferent to her father's absence and focused on the fights with her mother and on her girl friends at school.

They were all interested in boys and she was too, she said. Sara talked about which boys she liked the most. Although she did not go out on dates, boys always congregated on the front porch after school. Then her mother butted in or eavesdropped, she complained.

The focus on boys was intense, which was normal enough. But it seemed odd that she viewed her life as unchanged after her father's move away from home. Sara seemed anesthetized, out of touch with feelings she had buried—about the absence of her father and her long-distance relationship with him.

Soon, however, Sara began to talk more openly about this painful time. Through the year, Sara recalled, she seemed to endure frequent illnesses and accidents. Some would occur during her father's visits or soon after he left to return to his new home.

She would suffer, for instance, from recurring tonsillitis. When she stayed with her father and his new live-in girl friend, he would get up in the middle of the night to bring medicine to her. Once, Sara remembered, just after her father had visited, she was riding her bike to school, a soda bottle in her hand. Making a turn, her bike skidded and she was thrown to the pavement. Sara suffered a badly cut hand and the wound needed ten stitches. But Sara did not remember any pain. She did recall asking her mother, "Call Daddy quick and tell him to come back." When her mother refused, she became very upset.

The pattern of getting attention and affection by hurting herself, an unconscious process, had been established much earlier. When Sara had talked about the evening her father had carried her into the hospital emergency room with a sprained ankle, there was a special softness in her voice.

Her face seem to reflect her warm feelings about this special time she had had alone with her father, away from the family. She felt very important to him during this rare time she had his full attention.

Later, she became more keenly aware of her pain, her feelings of loss, and her anger toward her mother—and as she became more aware of the pain, her anger diminished.

A Helping Hand

The subject of Sara's suicidal threat came up later. Sara had been in a rage that morning, but she kept much of it buried inside of her. Despite her threats, Sara did not think she really wanted to die. What she wanted to do was put an end to the terrible feeling she had: of being alone and abandoned by everyone.

She vividly remembered her mother on the telephone, calling her therapist. In effect, Sara asked: "How much could she really care, getting on the phone with her shrink when I'm trying to kill myself?"

But Sara was more sympathetic when she thought about her mother as a real person. She agreed that her mother probably felt scared and uncertain what to do. Yes, she probably was doing the best she could, Sara guessed. And at that moment, all she could do was to turn to her own therapist. Maybe she felt just as vulnerable as Sara did.

Wasn't that possible?

"Yeah, I guess," said Sara.

Many parents do feel powerless in a time of crisis. It is understandable. But intervention is always possible. Here are some guidelines:

- Make it clear immediately that you are worried about your child's safety and well-being.

- Communicate that you do take threats of suicide seriously. Because of her own panic, for instance, Lily made a phone call to her therapist. But inadvertently, she reinforced her daughter's feeling that no one cared, that she was not important to her mother. To Sara, it made her mother seem even more distant.

For Sara, the ending was not tragic. But it might have been. The cut on her wrist was only minor, and it was apparent that she did not intend to kill herself. But such an act should be taken seriously. Many suicide victims do not intend to carry out the act but are not rescued in time. In Sara's case, the knife might have slipped and cut an artery, despite her own much less deadly scenario.

When Sara emerged from the bathroom, clutching her wrist, her mother screamed at her. Of course, Lily was upset and frightened. But for Sara, it was another turn of the screw, another rejection.

As a child, Sara had no sense that her mother was also a vulnerable human being, struggling to keep her own balance, overwhelmed by caring for two children without the daily emotional support of her husband. Sara was unaware of the stresses her mother felt.

But how serious was Sara's gesture?

Quite serious.

The episode was designed to serve at least two ends:

- Despite the angry words, Sara did in fact get her mother's undivided attention and an expression of caring.

• And Sara felt a sense of revenge—blaming her mother and seeing her mother suffer, the way Sara had suffered.

Sara had no memory of planning the act. In therapy, she thought she remembered wanting to escape—from her mother, her house, her life, "from the pain of it all."

She did not think she really wanted to be dead. And at the critical moment, she did not have the deep despair that is usually present in most cases of suicide, where the victim can see no other course of action.

For Sara, the episode was an irrational and angry act of striking out at her mother, teaching her a lesson, getting back for feeling so unloved, so unimportant, so abandoned, that she felt she did not exist at all.

Looking for Answers

What were the roots of Sara's crisis?

The year had been a tumultuous one for Sara, suddenly confronted by major changes in her life, all involving loss.

• Her father was gone, and little effort had been paid to prepare Sara and her sister for the breakup. Sara still felt closer to her father than her mother, especially now. And she missed him very much. Sara would have felt better if she had been encouraged to talk about those emotions.

• At home, her mother's new boy friend was on the scene. Sometimes Sara felt her mother was totally preoccupied with the new man in her life. While Sara claimed she had "no interest at all" in her mother's private life, she really felt she had lost her mother. She was also torn by ambivalent feelings toward her mother's new male friend. Sometimes she hated him. But at times she thought he was very attractive, younger looking than her father. Still, Sara complained, her mother always seemed too busy or too exhausted.

• Sara's father lived in another city, and he too had a new partner in his life, another upheaval for Sara. She did not like to think about that either.

These circumstances in themselves did not create the crisis in Sara's life. But Sara and her parents had trouble confronting these dramatic changes in their lives. Sara denied her hurt feelings, just as her parents had done in dealing with the subject of their divorce.

It was not easy for Sara's parents. Her mother, for instance, was upset about her impending divorce and the financial strain it would mean. She was unhappy about the loss of friends and social activities linked to her marriage. And while she had a new man in her life, he was not on hand to support her through the day-to-day anxieties of everyday living.

Sara's father also was preoccupied with new pressures. He too felt guilty about the family breakup. His visits with his children, twice a month, deprived him of the emotional satisfaction that he had once derived from his children. Trying to contend with his own turmoil, he was unaware of Sara's pain and how deeply she missed him.

Sara's feelings might have surfaced if her parents had been able to talk more openly about their decision to end their marriage and about the feelings that the breakup might stir up in the family.

Often, children can be given at least some of the reasons for their parents' decision to separate or to divorce. What is most important is that neither parent is made the scapegoat in the eyes of their children. In reality, both parents in a divorce share responsibility.

Later, it would have eased Sara's anxieties if she had been told exactly when and how often she would see her father in the future. Instead, Sara felt a wall of silence around her. Alone in her room, she sometimes felt like screaming, just to see what would happen. Sara, of course, was part of the silence. She was unable to come out and say: "Daddy, I'm going to miss you. Don't go away."

If her father had anticipated her feeling of loss, he might have made sure Sara knew that he would miss her too. For some parents, especially some fathers, such sentiments are sometimes hard to voice. But an expression of caring might have narrowed the abyss Sara felt.

Much later, Sara and her mother did begin to talk about

their feelings toward each other. In therapy, Sara examined her jealousy toward her mother's new boy friend and began to understand that her feelings were natural and acceptable. It was suggested that she could try to express these emotions to her mother, without catastrophe, and ultimately she did.

When children do have such negative feelings, their expression should be encouraged, not squelched—even though it is painful for parents to listen to their children express such anger or pain. For Sara, the suffering needed to be verbalized. Instead, she acted out a painful interior drama in the upstairs bathroom, with a carving knife.

Feeling Abandoned

Sara did not make the emotional puzzle a simple one for her parents. Her way of expressing pain was indirect and difficult to comprehend. She herself was unaware of her deeper feelings toward her absent father, her mother's private life, or the grim prospect of sharing her father with a strange new woman.

So Sara expressed herself with indifference rather than concern and, much of the time, her indifference came across as arrogance. Confronted with a monumental feeling of loss, she felt she had no one to turn to with her troubles—and she allowed lack of interest and indifference to successfully mask her anger. Such anger, Sara had been taught, was unacceptable in the rational world. So indifference was a way of denying pain and rejection.

Instead, her anger surfaced only in connection with such issues as curfews and clothing—clashes that began when her mother refused to buy her a fashionable brand of jeans, for instance, or to allow Sara to stay out past midnight with her friends.

The sense of crisis was heightened by biological timing. With the onset of puberty, Sara felt vague feelings of rivalry with her mother—just at a time when her external world was growing more unpredictable and chaotic.

Sara had always been "such a good girl," her mother said. Suddenly she was in state of rebellion and her mother was overwhelmed by the change. She wanted her little girl back. But Sara had reached adolescence, and the biological clock ticked on. With her father gone from the household at this crucial time, she felt more abandoned than ever.

For many children, indifference and quiet disdain is safer to communicate than pain and anger. Looking beyond the indifference and the resentment is an important first step that parents can take.

Staying in Touch

For children such as Sara, feelings of abandonment can be eased.

Occasionally, but not often enough, Sara did talk with her father on the phone. Later, she complained, her mother "always listened." And her father, she said, always seemed in such a hurry, maybe worrying over the cost of the long-distance calls.

She and her father did not write letters at all. The idea wasn't even raised until therapy sessions were underway. Then Sara began to write letters—just recounting what was happening to her in school and what her friends were like—and that did make her feel better. It provided the link she needed to feel closer to her father.

The presence of new suitors in the lives of parents and their impact on a child's life also can be handled more openly and directly, allowing the subject to be aired in a natural way, making it clear that the child's feelings count. It is helpful to remember that no matter how old a child is, even an adolescent such as Sara, he or she is likely to experience some feelings of being displaced and rejected.

Even if there is no response to these efforts to communicate, mothers and fathers at least can continue to be available emotionally. In Sara's case, she was so disagreeable, so complaining, so aloof, that her mother avoided any approach, such as asking her for assistance around the house or taking part in mother-daughter activities.

Sara's mother certainly meant well, but in trying to protect her troubled daughter, she reinforced Sara's feelings of rejection. And Sara felt even more isolated. No one, after all, gave her any candid account about the nature of a marriage breakup and what difficulties it would bring. It would have given Sara a chance to vent some of her anxieties if someone had said: "I know it might be really scary for a while, feeling like you're losing your daddy."

Such expressions would have allowed Sara to deal with her pain and fears with greater ease, because they echoed what she truly felt. But those realities were dealt with later, after Sara's suicide scare brought her feelings into the open. When the therapy sessions began, Sara was stubborn, holding onto her feelings of misery as if they were all she had in the world.

So she held up her guard. Inside, she felt that if she really got angry at her mother, she would be abandoned for good. And to show her pain was to be vulnerable. Her show of indifference made her feel stronger. At least she could defend herself.

In her therapy sessions, Sara learned she could allow herself to be vulnerable. In one of the final sessions, Sara and her mother came in together.

"Are you angry?" the therapist asked, when Sara swiveled her chair toward the wall.

"I'm not angry," Sara said.

"Are you sure?"

"Yeah, I'm sure," she said.

"Well, I wonder why you're not looking at me or your mother?" her therapist said.

Sara turned and looked at her mother for the first time that day.

"Well, it seems to me, Sara, that when your feelings hurt, you act as though you are very angry . . . like the time your father moved away.

Sara looked flushed.

"Yes, it is," Sara said. "That's how I act."

"I guess you feel stronger when you're angry," the therapist said.

Sara nodded, and she and her mother looked at each other and embraced warmly. It was something new for both of them—a more direct and honest way of communicating.

119

Fred: Off to college

Fred never showed any signs of stress.

The youngest of three children, he was just two years old when his parents were divorced. Through his grade school and high school years, he made friends easily, loved sports, and enjoyed his classes. On weekends, he saw his father regularly, and a loving and supportive relationship evolved over the years.

Fred was still seventeen when he entered college. An above-average student, he looked forward to the challenge and the freedom of college life. Although he had never lived away from home before, he had no reservations about attending an out-of-town school, and he seemed to relish the idea of being on his own for the first time.

After considering a number of distant colleges, he finally chose to attend a small college in New Jersey, only a few hours away by car. In the first few months on campus, he seemed to be making a mature adjustment, coping well with this first separation from home.

He telephoned his mother occasionally but not too often. He was very busy, he said, and probably would not come home for a visit until the Thanksgiving holiday. In his infrequent letters—notes, really—he was upbeat about campus social life: dorm living, new friends, intramural sports. He did not mention class work often, but he was "keeping up."

There were no signals of loneliness or isolation, feelings experienced by many teenagers during the first months of college life. Fred sounded very happy—and his mother was relieved.

Then, during the last week in October, Fred was injured playing touch football. Nothing serious. Colliding with another player, he suffered a painfully sprained left wrist. Since he was right-handed, the injury did not hinder his school work. But Fred was upset. In all the years of rough-and-tumble sports at home, he had never been hurt.

Fred telephoned home after the accident, complaining that he would not be able to play any sports for the rest of the fall season. "What a shame," his mother Paula said. She was sympathetic and asked if Fred needed anything special. "No, I'm fine really, just annoyed," he said.

Fred came home for Thanksgiving and seemed relaxed. His wrist was still bandaged, but he had been able to jog in the mornings. In fact, he joked, he was having a run of bad luck. Just before the holiday break, he had failed to notice a car making a tight left-hand turn on a campus road, and the car's fender just grazed him. But he was unhurt. Not even scratched. Just unlucky, he guessed.

The third accident came in December, and this time Fred was scared. He had been playing basketball and injured his back while attempting a difficult off-balance lay-up. The gym supervisor stepped in and Fred had to wait thirty minutes, laying motionless on his back, before an ambulance arrived from the local hospital.

The news was good and bad: No serious damage had been done. But Fred would have to wear a neck brace for at least three months.

His mother arrived that evening, and the next day she went with Fred to see a specialist. "You've had a rough year," she said before Fred entered the doctor's examining room.

She resisted the temptation to follow him in, reminding herself that Fred was now a young adult and had been away from home for four months. She did not want him to think that she was babying him. Then, when he emerged from the office, they had a remarkable exchange.

"The doctor says I've really got to lay low for a while," Fred said. "No dancing or playing ball until the summer."

His mother was silent.

Walking back to the car, she fought back a powerful temptation to tell Fred what she thought these unexpected accidents were all about. There was more silence.

Then Fred mused, more to himself than to his mother, "Gee, wouldn't it be strange if I made this happen, so I'd have to stay home and study?" With so many parties, he said, it really had been hard to concentrate on school work. "Wouldn't it be funny if I really got hurt purposely?"

"It sure would be," Fred's mother agreed, glad she had

kept silent at the crucial moment, not offering the insight herself.

Catching the Signals

Bravo for such instincts.

Fred's mother had suppressed her urge to lecture: "Maybe you needed to lay low, as the doctor put it." If she had stepped in prematurely, she might have sounded an unnecessarily negative chord. It might have seemed punitive, and it might have made Fred feel like a adolescent who had to defend himself or like a little boy who was accused of being reckless.

Silence gave Fred a moment to explore his own feelings. And so he did. He was able to experience a sense of self-discovery instead of feeling that another theory was being forced on him by an adult.

Fred did ride out this critical period, and his accident-prone behavior diminished. Later, talking with some of her friends who also had teenage children, Fred's mother recalled her son's mishaps during his freshman year. Two questions were raised:

- What could parents do to ease their children's feelings of separation before they went off to an out-of-town college?

- What could they do when a crisis arose, such as the series of accidents Fred suffered?

Fred's experience was part of a familiar pattern among young people who have left home for the first time. Even though young people may choose to leave home and are eager to begin college, they may resent leaving a safe, secure place and may feel that they are being pushed into an alien world before they are ready. Such a feeling can lead to depression and self-destructive or self-defeating behavior. The fear, often unrecognized by parents and by the teenager himself, is that he is really not able to care for himself or to function independently. For Fred, his series of accidents brought some subtle benefits:

1. By hurting himself, Fred evoked more attention from his mother. Didn't she rush to the school when she was needed? So the accidents, especially the most serious one, allowed Fred to feel in close touch with his mother without seeing himself as a "baby."

2. The campus accidents rendered maternal attention acceptable. Fred, after all, didn't ask his mother to come to the campus, like some small child who was lonely or needed his mommy!

3. Fred found an acceptable rationale to channel his energies to his school work. Now he had time to get down to the serious stuff of college life, the scary business of preparing for the future, an occupation, a livelihood—issues more connected to adulthood than childhood.

Still, Fred's mother wondered: Could she have prevented this outbreak of accident-prone behavior?

How to Help

Fred's accidents, after all, were not the fault of Fred's mother or father. But steps can be taken early to make a child's passage into adulthood less painful and, therefore, less dangerous. For example:

- Talk, talk, talk—about feelings. Before your children leave home, go into detail about the separation and what it might feel like. Recall your own experiences and the days and nights you missed being home, missed your old friends, missed walking on familiar streets—even when you didn't miss your parents. And if your son or daughter doesn't want to talk about it? Talk anyway!

- Stay in touch. Once he or she leaves home, send packages and letters. Make phone calls. Never mind the disclaimers and the complaints. There might be many protests of independence and much bravado. You may agree that phone calls aren't mandatory. But if you want to make them—one call every week or two, especially at first, is hardly excessive or inappropriate.

- Pack something familiar when your son or daughter leaves home for the first time. It might be a lamp, a bedspread, a favorite poster, something familiar from his or her room.

- Choose your words with care. If your children say you make them feel child-like, examine your own feelings and your rhetoric. How do you sound on the phone? Are you infantilizing? But there is no reason to avoid calling to say "Hello" or "How are you doing?" It doesn't have to be a third-degree or a cross-examination. Remember: The intent is to make your children feel better. So keep in touch, even when suddenly grown-up college students don't initiate the contact.

During the first weeks Fred was away, for instance, his mother was puzzled by all the bravado. Fred seemed to be doing so well. He called only twice a month, but then, he would have seen himself as childish if he had called more often. A bit of strategy, an end-run around Fred's sincere declarations of independence, might have been useful. For instance:

1. Visits to the campus might be set up in advance. They might allay underlying anxieties—to know that you care and are coming for a visit two or three times a year, whether your student likes it or not.

2. Don't be afraid to take the initiative in dealing with absent children. Adolescents, beset by ambivalent feelings, are often afraid to show their neediness. So make it clear: You want to make the visit, not because you're being asked to but because you plan to enjoy it.

3. Most of all, don't push. Stay tuned in to all the signals. If your son or daughter does not feel prepared to leave home for college, it is crucial that you don't force the issue. For children beset with separation anxieties, concentration on studies might be difficult and going away to college could be a waste of time, energy, and money.

Remember that there is nothing wrong with a breather

when your children are not ready to leave home for a distant campus. There are many alternatives:

- A junior college in your own community. It might ease the transition from high school to campus.

- A university within commuting distance. This too could serve to lessen the pangs of separation.

- A genuine sabbatical. Even at seventeen or eighteen, some adolescents benefit from a year off from school, taking at a job in the workaday world before returning to the tension of study and classes and career thinking.

Of course, separation anxieties aren't the only reason for balking at college. He or she simply might be unready to face the rigors and the discipline of academic life.

So if your son or daughter wants to stay home or delay enrollment in a college—pay attention to the signals. They may save both you and your child suffering later.

Asking Questions

Fred, of course, had no desire to postpone college or to stay at home. But after his series of accidents, there were grounds for concern. What can parents do in this situation? Here are some questions to ask yourself:

1. How did your children deal with separations in earlier stages of their lives? These patterns sometimes repeat.

2. Is something different happening? In the case of Fred, who never hurt himself before, so it seemed.

3. Listen carefully to the details. If you feel you aren't getting enough information, ask direct questions. Don't be afraid to broach the subject:

   Was everyone wearing the proper equipment?

   Was the activity supervised?

Was anyone using drugs at the time?

Were other students getting hurt?

Were unnecessary or unreasonable risks involved?

4. Most of all, try to remember your own teen years. Adolescence is a painful time—so painful, in fact, that many parents tend to forget how upsetting it really was. In part, it is painful because adolescents are trying to develop their own identity, to break away from home and parents, and to figure out ways to feel safe and secure about themselves.

But at the same time—even as they try to break away—they really don't want to. At least, a part of them needs to hold on, to feel safe and protected, to be cared for—just as their parents might have felt when they were the same age. Often adolescents find such feelings unacceptable. And parents, forgetting how painful those years were for them, can find it difficult to empathize with their own children.

Instead, it is easy to become annoyed with children who cling too tightly. Perhaps the gesture reminds parents of their own neediness. Other parents may become angry when their offspring move away too readily. Parents too can feel abandoned or valueless, unneeded and unappreciated. So it helps to remember their own past. If they could conjure up the insecure child within themselves, they might be able to empathize with their own children.

Needy After All These Years

This period can mean hard times for both parents and their adolescents. Beneath the bravado and the protest, teenagers still can be needy and dependent. The more bravado, the more dependent adolescents may be. But there are ways for parents to lighten the burden. For instance:

1. Acknowledge with approval every attempt your children make toward independence, no matter how small it is.

2. Talk about your own ambivalence when you were a teenager, how hard it was for you when you left home at the same age. If you can't conjure up the memories, talk to relatives or old friends who might provide clues to the past, to enable you to recall your own teen days.

3. Remember that you are not the enemy, even though your child may cast you in that role. You are, after all, not in the midst of an adversarial proceeding. You are trying to assist your children to move away as successfully as possible—and in a way that will leave the door open, with emotional connections unsevered.

Remember also that becoming angry at parents is part of the process of separating. But angry children are usually in pain. So despite their anger, it helps to respond to their hurt. Often, that is difficult to do. At times, it seems easier for parents to allow themselves to be cast in the role of enemy, because it allows them to become angry too. Being angry can seem more comfortable at times than the pain of losing children to inevitable adulthood.

It helps to call up memories of your children, when they were age two, for instance, and in the midst of a temper tantrum. Full of pain and frustration, they wanted to be held and soothed. In some ways, that is what the hurting adolescent often wants but cannot ask for. In some cases, parents do not allow themselves to comfort their teenagers physically. A hug can be reassuring—but parents can also offer comfort with words.

"I can remember feeling the way you feel."

"I know how really frustrating things can get sometimes."

"Something like that happened to me once, and I hated my parents for a whole semester."

It is not easy to cast such lines of support. Unable to empathize, mothers and fathers may react to teenage rage too personally. Putting one's disappointment aside is hard to do. But all the sound and fury is usually ineffective and incommunicative, as meaningful as scolding a tearful two-year-old in the midst of a tantrum.

It can be difficult. But when mothers and fathers forget how painful their own childhoods were, the difficulty is heightened. And parents will be even more helpless in the face of their children's fear and pain and anger.

Looking Back—And Inward

At a crucial moment, Fred's mother was able to remember something from her own girlhood. She was aware that Fred had been neglecting his school work. Sports and dances and dating were too much fun. Fred was feeling free, away from home and surrounded by a buffet of good times. And what a good way to deny the future, to postpone the reality of having to grow up. Fred's mother recalled that she too had once felt that way: that she was quite happy not to think about growing up.

"I wanted to tell Fred that I suspected he was going through a similar experience," she recalled. Instead, she remained silent, allowing Fred himself to recognize that something mysterious might be going on inside of him.

It would be strange if somehow he had orchestrated the series of accidents, he mused after the third mishap. In a way, he was conceding to himself: "This is not a good thing I'm doing to myself." But it was even more important that the feeling came from within, that he recognized a more mature aspect of himself.

Fred's mother felt very good that she had remained silent. "If I had said anything, he probably would have denied it." Instead, Fred was able to express himself—to make his own discovery. Fred's mother let her son come to his own conclusion. She recognized that she had no real power to tell Fred what he ought to feel. All she could do was tell him how she had once felt. And Fred's own powers of discovery made him feel responsible for what was going on in his life. It was a good response in a time of crisis.

LEAVING HOME

For children of all ages, separation is a real test—from the first day of kindergarten to the first day of college.

Feelings of separation and abandonment can trigger frightening and often dangerous emotional pyrotechnics, expressed through crises of mysterious illness and unexplained accidents, suicidal feelings, drug abuse, and learning problems.

There are times, of course, when young people seem to be asking for trouble. They drive too fast. They take risks on the playing field and with sex. They seem to thrive on hazardous living. There are those, of course, who come close to the edge—relishing the most risky challenges while mountain climbing, surfing, or skiing.

Most often, this behavior reflects hardy competitiveness and the need for adventure. But for some, it may connect to other parts of their psyche—to deep and masked feelings of depression, frequently stemming from a fear of separation and abandonment.

Some adolescents, such as Edie—who ran away from home when she was not yet seventeen—appear ready to handle separation.

Some, such as Cathy—who found herself vulnerable to the lure of a cult group—find the first year away from home a painful one.

And some face unexpected crisis and challenge from parents when they feel ready to move out of their homes and into a place of their own. In the eyes of their parents they may be too young to go. In their own minds they may be too old to live at home. But beneath it all, there are fears of separation and feelings of abandonment for both parents and children. These feelings must be faced if a warm and loving relationship is to extend into the future.

Edie: A teen mother

In her dreamy girlhood, Edie would sit alone in the school cafeteria, conjuring up her future. She was only thirteen, but the visions of adulthood danced brightly in her head. She was going to be free!

She'd leave home after high school and become a nurse or a flight attendant. She'd live anywhere she wanted to. She'd have a neat apartment with her best girl friend. They'd go out with lots of boys, not worrying about getting married, like her mother did, so young. She would escape prying parents and curfews and rules, rules, rules.

It almost came true for Edie.

Edie was not promiscuous, but just after her sixteenth birthday she had sex with her boy friend for the first time. When they broke up in the spring, Edie was very upset. For a time, she went to bed with a half-dozen boys, but it didn't feel very good. She felt hurt and rejected and wasn't sure what she was doing. Then she decided to take off from home and see the world.

Still sixteen, she quit high school and took off for Europe with two boys who had finished school. She traveled economy-class, hitchhiking from Paris to Athens, in search of freedom and . . . something.

Now Edie is eighteen, and part of the old dream is a reality. She does share an apartment with a girl friend. But she's back in her old home town, living only a mile from her parents' home—and she has an infant of her own. Motherhood at nineteen was never part of her girlhood dream.

A Special Case

Edie, however, was not a victim of unwanted pregnancy: She was a mother more by design than by accident; she was single more by choice than by chance; and she was not sorry.

In the few years since she left high school, her life had undergone momentous changes. She became more serious. She was no longer on a sexual rollercoaster, and she was concerned about her future. Getting pregnant when she was eighteen was the most unexpected turn of events.

About the baby, she reached a decision almost immediately: Abortion was something she found unappealing, even though she felt the right to have an abortion was a matter of personal choice. An imperfect marriage, mandated by a pregnancy, was a dismal thought. And giving up her child for adoption was not even contemplated.

So Edie became a full-time mother, although her parents did not accept her decision and refused to help her. They remained angry that their daughter had "thrown away her life."

Edie and her girl friend, who was divorced and also had a child, devised a communal arrangement, sharing welfare checks and food stamps and rent expenses. They converted their living room into a nursery for the two children, and they shared the bedroom, using sleeping bags when they moved in because they could not afford furniture. They decided on the room arrangement because they felt the apartment did not have to be turned into a pair of "mother-and-child" bedrooms, each with a baby atmosphere.

After rent and food expenses, there was little left over for two young women and two children; it was not a joy ride, no matter what critics of welfare aid say. "Sometimes," Edie recalled, "I think the world wanted us to be unhappy."

But Edie decided to fight the stereotype of the unwed mother: that there was something tragic or sad about raising her child alone, that single mothers were somehow less worthy than mothers who were divorced or separated or widowed.

Edie's parents were both furious and ashamed that their

daughter refused to marry when she was eighteen and pregnant. To them she was still a little girl. The decision, her father felt, was not hers alone to make. After all, the father of her unborn child had been willing to marry her, "to do the right thing," as her father put it.

Looking back on her choice, Edie recalled that she felt that neither she nor the father of her child was mature enough to marry. They did not love each other and had been casual traveling companions on Edie's trip across Europe. "Getting married was not something I would have wanted to punish him with—with that kind of responsibility when he was not ready for it. And I wasn't ready to be a wife."

Edie had talked about going back to school, but without her parents' support, it was impossible. Perhaps she could go back to school part-time while sharing child-raising duties, but Edie had to postpone that plan. Getting married was certainly another viable option, and she looked upon her living arrangement as temporary. Marriage, she thought, was desirable and inevitable, but not immediately. Meanwhile, Edie knew that she had several years of poverty ahead of her.

Sometimes she felt that she would never get off welfare. When she was nineteen, it seemed so unfair—having a newborn baby to worry about when other kids were just starting college. And sometimes, Edie said, "you think that the baby needs socks and even buying something like that would just about break our bank."

But she was not unhappy. She enjoyed having her own apartment, even if she did share it. She liked the idea of being her own boss, sitting in her kitchen on a fall afternoon and watching the leaves fall. On such days, she felt secure and even lucky.

"Now if I get married I can pick someone who is good for me and my son," she said. "But I don't have to feel that anyone else is the center of my life. I've got a family now. I'm my own center now."

She had been taught by her parents that having a child outside marriage was wrong. "But I thought I was doing the right thing. I didn't feel hurt when people said nasty things or when my parents criticized. I never felt guilty, but I worried.

Was I going to be left alone in a corner? Was everyone going to ignore me? That was part of the fear."

Running Away

At seventeen, Edie had felt the need for freedom. It had been building since she was twelve or thirteen. "There was something I had to do, to take off and see what kind of a world it was out there. Leaving home seemed the only way out. And I was always a little rebellious. When my father told me to stay in the house, I went out. I was told not to smoke and I smoked anyway. But I never got into any trouble."

Still, there were some bad fights at home.

"Once when I was fourteen and getting interested in boys, my father yelled at me: You're probably gonna get pregnant by the time you're eighteen. He was very angry about something, but I was really hurt. I mean, I had never even thought about doing anything with a boy. But it's odd, because it turned out he was right."

So a month after high school let out, she and two friends took off for Europe, using money she had earned at an after-school job. In France, she met a boy who lived in a neighboring village back home, and they started traveling together. Later in the year, in Athens, she became pregnant.

She had not taken any birth control precautions. "I guess I was one of those people who just hopes everything will be all right. Maybe deep down, I wanted to have a child. I don't know."

When she became pregnant, Edie decided to return home. She recalled thinking, "Maybe this is wrong, . . . but it wasn't the baby that was wrong. Maybe I went against my parents' code, about sleeping with anyone before I was married, but everyone does that. So what do I do? Have an abortion? Get married? Give the kid away?"

Edie decided that none of the options was right for her. She had mixed feelings, of course: fear, anxiety, confusion. "I knew I would have the baby, but it was just such a dramatic change in my life and I was still eighteen . . . Anyway, I was

133

glad the running in circles was over." Having a child was a message to stop running, Edie said.

Edie's Parents

Edie's parents discovered her pregnancy by accident. A letter from a girl friend arrived at her parents' home, mentioning the pregnancy. Now, Edie thinks she may have left the letter on a table deliberately, just so her parents would find out: an easier way of breaking the news to them.

"It was the way my life had always been with my parents. Having them find out things accidently. I always would get caught at anything I did. But I could never come straight out and talk to them." One of her friends even volunteered to break the news to her father and mother, but the letter did the job. They were stunned.

Her mother broke the silence. She and Edie had to talk about the problem, she said. Her father said nothing. Even a year later, Edie has never really talked to him about getting pregnant and having a child.

"I know they wanted me to get married, no matter what I felt. Even though I told them I didn't want to live with him. They wanted me to talk to a priest. They told me that what I was doing was wrong." For the sake of her parents, Edie learned to lie about the baby.

"I'm really happy with him. I feel he's made me a real person and I think my life is a lot easier than being unhappily married. I wish my parents understood. It wouldn't be so lonely. And the lying bothers me. Like running into old teachers or neighbors on my parents' street. They say—'Oh I didn't know you were married'—when they see the baby. My mother told everyone I was married and separated. Well, I can't see hurting my parents by spilling out the truth, but it makes me feel like I've done something dirty."

Even at her baby shower, she recalled, one of her friends suggested that she put up her son for adoption. "At a baby shower! Can you imagine!"

Without parental support, Edie felt a sense of control over her life that she had never experienced before. It made her parents even more angry. "For the first time, I felt I could say exactly how I was going to deal with situations. I didn't feel that way when I was with my baby's father, and I never felt that way when I was with my parents."

Her parents, Edie said, refused to recognize that she was a different person. To them she was still a teenager. "But I was very different," she said, "I'd become a mother."

Facing Realities

In trying to shape the lives of their children, parents run the risk of estrangement, especially at times when their wishes run counter to those of their children, as in Edie's case.

Later, Edie recalled the time that her father angrily had predicted her early pregnancy. The event, after all, was not part of a conscious plan or strategy.

But children like Edie, struggling to find an adult identity of their own, are likely to react rather than to act on their own. In effect, Edie was prompted to act in exactly the way her parents feared. Inadvertently, another arena of defiance was created and Edie jumped in to assert herself.

Edie's parents were very hurt, of course. Their daughter was so different from the one they believed they had raised. But they might have eased tensions between Edie and themselves by recognizing that the choice their daughter ultimately made—to have her child—was in response to a very real crisis.

She had rejected the choice of abortion. A forced marriage was unappealing and unrealistic. Adoption seemed unnecessary. Edie made the choice she felt most comfortable with, a decision she felt best for herself and her child.

It might have helped if Edie had been applauded for her courage and her determination. Indeed, the idea of motherhood out of wedlock was difficult for Edie's parents to accept. But they were not asked to condone their daughter's action— only to be there, to offer emotional support.

Even though Edie's parents felt that her decision to have her child was not in her best interests at the time, they could not impose their wishes and values without the risk of driving their daughter even further away. And that is what happened.

So the saddest part of Edie's story is about loss. In a time of crisis, her mother and father deprived themselves of an opportunity to support their daughter's efforts to move toward independence and an adult identity. And they also deprived themselves of the joy of a new role, as grandparents.

Edie did leave home, and her parents were saddened by her choice. But when a child leaves home, relationships with parents do change.

To prepare for change, parents have work to do too. They must be ready to feel their own pain over the loss of their child—and ready to embrace the developing young adult who returns in her stead.

Edie, the young woman—still a teenager but also a young adult—might have been a welcome addition to the lives of her parents, an enrichment even in the midst of crisis. When Edie's parents felt embarrassed by her decision to have a child out of wedlock, communication with their daughter broke down. But Edie was a survivor. No doubt, her parents must have provided her with some of the strength she displayed in her firm decision making.

Adolescents like Edie present a special challenge to parents, making an unspoken demand that their parents grow past their own wishes and needs and accept them for what they really are—even when they are most saddened by the choices their children make for themselves.

For all parents, experiencing these changes in their relationship with adolescent children entails a natural process of grieving. But along the way, mothers and fathers can gain strength from each other and from other parents who have already experienced that special loss of a child—leaving home for the first time and doing so in a way they did not expect and found hard to accept.

Cathy: The lure of the cult

Cathy's troubles began when she was seventeen and left home for the first time. A year earlier she had entered a good coeducational prep school in New England as a junior. It had been her parents' idea, but Cathy was happy about the move.

Shy but bright, she was eager to learn, and she worried about getting into one of the "better" colleges. In the summer after her junior year, however, after living away from home for a year, Cathy stunned her parents by deciding to drop out of school.

Just after her seventeenth birthday, after several weeks of cryptic letters and abbreviated telephone calls, she revealed that she had joined a campus cult group, active at a nearby college. She had become deeply involved with the cult's "message" and she was caught up in new feelings of intense camaraderie.

So just after the school year ended, she drove to California with four members of the group, joining in a summer of street action: seeking new recruits and raising money to support the cult's commune outside a small town.

How It Began

Cathy grew up in a suburban town just outside New York City, the youngest of four children. She had attended a parochial grade school, but by the time she entered high school she had slipped away from the orthodoxy of her childhood and felt turned off by organized religion.

"I was still sixteen when I went off to boarding school," she said later. "For the first time, I was really away from home, from my family and all my friends. High school was a pretty big success—I did well in class, was a cheerleader, worked on the school paper, had lots of friends."

But, she added, she always felt much younger than her classmates. "I didn't date very much, and as far as sex was concerned, I didn't think I'd sleep with anyone until I got married. I felt a lot of confusion about sex. I didn't want to do anything."

So going to an out-of-town prep school was a culture shock. "Suddenly I was alone. There was a lot of social pressure. Some of the girls were terribly sophisticated or they acted like it. And some were pretty experienced with boys.

Everyone talked about going home on off-campus weekends, going to parties, getting drunk, going to bed with somebody, anybody."

Cathy felt left out. "I wasn't into sex or getting stoned or drunk. Also my roommate and I were just a perfect mismatch, and I didn't seem to be able to talk to any of the other girls on my corridor."

At school, Cathy felt vulnerable and on guard. Some days, she missed home so much she cried, hiding her tears from her roommate. But her parents seemed so upbeat and excited about Cathy's adventures at a new and prestigious school that she kept her miseries to herself.

She had been sad before. When she was four, she was devastated when her teenage sister Jenny was killed in a car accident. Jenny had been like a second mother to her. Then, the following year, Cathy began kindergarten, leaving home for the first time, another wrenching experience. Now, at school, these lonely and painful memories returned.

But one weekend evening, a few months after school began, she attended a play at a nearby college. There she met a very friendly girl named Susanne. A freshman in college, Susanne was eighteen, a year and a half older than Cathy.

"In the theater lobby during intermission, Susanne struck up a conversation with one of the girls from my dorm. She had a big smile and she sounded very smart. The play ended early and it was a Saturday night so we all sat around after the show. It was a new experience: a serious discussion. This was what college girls were supposed to be like," Cathy thought.

So when Susanne suggested that the prep school girls visit her campus the next weekend, Cathy was all for the idea. It was a welcome change. The next Saturday afternoon, Cathy took the local bus to Susanne's school. In the dorm, Susanne and her roommates were in the middle of a complicated discussion about religion and philosophy, far over Cathy's head. Cathy loved it.

"Susanne was so sure of everything. God's message, she said, was a beautiful diamond that could be split in only one way or else it would be ruined."

Before driving Cathy back to her school, Susanne picked out some books she said Cathy might find interesting. "Maybe we can talk about them sometime," she said. But it wasn't Susanne's views about the universe that attracted Cathy.

"She seemed so interested in everything I thought and she accepted me for what I was, without any demands or expectations. At least, that's how it felt."

The following weekend, Susanne dropped by just to say hello and to ask if Cathy had had a chance to read any of the books. They had a long talk. Cathy felt very special. About two weeks later, Susanne telephoned Cathy's dorm one night and invited her to a Saturday afternoon get-together, a kind of non-denominational "study group," she called it.

Cathy was beginning to think of Susanne as her only friend, and the thought pleased her. It was like having an older sister again, someone who was worldly and cared what she thought.

At the Saturday meeting, Cathy was overwhelmed with good feelings. "I discovered that whatever I was interested in, everyone else also seemed interested in. Without lifting a finger, I had solved the biggest problem about being away from home—finding people like myself, people who thought and felt just the way I did about everything. It was paradise."

There were no hints that strings were attached.

"Their image was so all-American, so clean-cut, you'd never suspect anything," Cathy said later in therapy. "There was no talk about communal living or chanting in the street. Most of the boys and girls were pretty young. A few were in high school like me, but most were college freshman. I got the message that most of them disapproved of wild stuff, sex and drugs and the like, and that was a relief."

But the most memorable moment of the session was the "love-bombing." Or so it was called. "I felt total acceptance from everyone around me. They seemed so warm and sincere. There was hugging and touching and kissing, but it wasn't sexual. It was pure affection. There wasn't a trace of the awkwardness of meeting someone for the first time, like on a date."

There was also a formal side to the meeting: a reading from the Bible and a lecture by an older woman. Then there were some songs and prayers, and people thanked God for blessing them. It was very unthreatening, except for a brief episode at the end, when people seemed to speak in a strange way.

Later, Cathy learned that they were speaking in tongues, as they called it. It was a way in which the voice of the Holy Spirit emerged from within them, one of the older students told her. Later, Cathy herself learned to speak in tongues, and the technique was mind-blowing. "We'd practice all the time and it blotted out everything else in your head."

There was also some talk of courses in "spiritual truths" that cost $200. But Cathy was not ready to ask her parents for extra money or to talk about her new friends. Still, she was eager to return to school after the winter recess. Spending more and more time on weekends with Susanne and her group, she found herself surrounded by a new community of friendship.

"They all seemed so eager to know what I was thinking, and they wanted to be with me almost every moment. Sometimes, they'd visit my school in the afternoon, just to sit around and talk. I began to feel I was never alone." Her friends urged her to take the course in "spiritual truths," and one weekend, she and a group of other new recruits were shown a film in which members of the group told how their newly found beliefs had changed their lives.

When the film ended, Cathy signed up for the course, a forty-hour extravaganza. And within weeks, she began to help recruit some of her own classmates. Then, when spring vacation began, she convinced her parents to let her remain at school, to write some papers during the break, she told them— and she began the indoctrination course.

"It was exhausting. We'd listen to cassettes for three hours at a time. The sessions were eight hours each day for five days. There was no duress, but it was strongly suggested that we not even get up to go to the bathroom. We had a few ten-minute breaks. I quickly accepted what I was told, and whatever the voice on the cassette claimed to be—a Hindu or a Greek scholar or whatever—I'd believe it. When passages of the Bible were explained, I'd accept it. If I doubted anything, I was told it was not my fault. I was just thinking the wrong way. If I just followed God's message, I'd be fulfilled. That's what they told me."

Looking back, Cathy added: "I realize now that there was no message. The message was mind control."

That spring, Cathy felt euphoric. Life seemed so simple, so untroubled. Everything made sense. She lost interest in school work that had fascinated her the previous semester—reading Homer and Keats and European history. All she wanted to do was to spread the word, "the good news about God." Just the way Susanne had when Cathy first met her.

Preoccupied with the extracurricular world of the spirit, Cathy's grades began to slip. Instead of studying, she'd find herself in intense arguments with her classmates about religion. Her intensity gave her somewhat of an odd-ball image in her dorm, and she felt more isolated than ever. She barely passed her final exams.

Upon returning home, there were explosive arguments with her parents. Cathy felt that she had grasped an ultimate truth, and she could not understand why her parents were so alienated. So in early July she took off for California with four members of the group. They stayed at one of the group's camps. Later, she recalled: "I felt like we were all brothers and sisters." She decided to postpone plans to return to school for her senior year in the fall, and she telephoned the news to her parents.

The next day, her parents began a nonstop drive to California. A week later, at the cult's campsite, Cathy and her parents met briefly and Cathy felt reassured.

"I thought I'd convinced them that it was a good idea, my taking some time off from school, to find out more about myself. They gave me their blessings. It was a great relief. At least they understood. Or so I thought."

The next afternoon, while Cathy was reading on the lawn, two of her brothers and a cousin appeared at the commune.

They said they were on a trip up the coast and had just stopped by to say hello. Cathy did not give their explanation a second thought.

"I don't think I perceived much reality at that point. It really was odd, the three of them being there only one day after my parents had left, but I didn't even think about it."

As they were leaving, Cathy walked with them to their car. Another brother was waiting. Suddenly, Cathy was pushed into the back seat of the car and they all drove off. It all happened so quickly. Cathy remembers that she did not feel angry at the time, just confused.

"I was sure I could convince them that I was doing the right thing. If only things would slow down, I'd explain. Then we could all live here together." A half hour later, she saw her parents and she understood. She was being kidnapped by her family.

"I felt I had two choices: to run away and really destroy my relationship with my parents and my family, people I loved—or go home and try to work things out. So I went home with my parents."

Back home, the euphoric high began to recede. Separation from the cult/commune life was a first step in the process of breaking away. "My parents took me on a short vacation. At home, my parents would not let me leave the house alone. Members of the group called, but I wasn't allowed to talk with them. A month or so later, I stopped reading the Bible. My parents had hired a professional deprogrammer, and he had been talking with me every day."

During the next few months, the deprogrammer was the first of many people who talked with Cathy, including a therapist and a network of ex-members of cults she met through a local clinic. But in the early weeks, she often slept 11 or 12 hours a day, feeling disoriented at times, not sure what was going on. It took more than a year for feelings of depression to pass.

The following year, Cathy enrolled in another school, college-bound once again. At times, she missed her old friends and the feeling of being accepted without question. "That's hard to give up, as hard as drugs, maybe."

Spotting a Cult

Cathy did not really understand the emotional pressures playing on her psyche. Cults, after all, vary in size and form. Some are small sects, whereas others are part of international movements. Some reflect traditional forms of mysticism. Others tend to be eccentric, promoting innovative beliefs based, in one case, on the transmigration of souls in flying saucers.

But often, a cluster of traits is found:

- There may be a "living leader," a self-appointed messianic figure who offers some revealed truth and promises immunity from disaster to members of the cult.

- Often, outsiders may be barred, creating a sense of mystery and isolation within the cult group.

- At times, double standards may be set about sex, in which sexuality within the group is rigidly restricted but sex is used to recruit new members.

One of the signals, as in Cathy's case, is the demand that members radically change their way of life, giving up relationships with family and friends, working full-time for the good of the group.

Most therapists feel that cult members can be helped. But reaching them early is crucial. Most therapists also warn that deprogramming is an inexact practice, at times performed by untrained or insensitive people. Some methods are controversial, questionable, harsh, and on the legal borderline. Deprogramming can be effective, but it should be part of a program of professional counseling, perhaps with former cult members participating.

The most difficult task is to get returnees to see that the cult's lure—a magical cure for all life's problems—can be a self-destructive fraud. It is also crucial for parents to avoid blaming their children.

Many young people return with identities so fragile that they cannot make even the simplest decision, such as what to wear or what to read. Losing the community that gave such unquestioning support, these returnees go through a period in which they perceive "normal" life as empty and meaningless.

Often young people leave cult groups voluntarily. At other times, they return home after a debriefing experience. But in either case, psychotherapy often is in order to aid former cult members to establish realistic methods to separate from home and parents later. As Cathy put it, "Being accepted is hard to give up."

Can Parents Help?

The cult question is both frightening and puzzling for the parents of adolescents. Why are some children so vulnerable, while others remain untouched? The emotional makeup of the young person might offer some clues, and parents might examine their child's psychological history:

- How did the child cope with stress at various ages?

- Did he or she find early separation difficult?

- Was the child overwhelmed by loss, such as a death in the family or the breakup of a friendship?

As in Cathy's case, young people who become involved with cults are often going through a period of separation and loss. Like Cathy, they feel defenseless and vulnerable. They cannot take the initiative to connect, in a meaningful way, with the new people in their lives. Until they are suddenly comforted by a group of supportive, uncritical newcomers— such as members of a cult—they feel empty and unvalued.

The cult group provides a reassuring message:

You are not alone.

You are worthwhile.

You are one of us.

The impact of the message can be stunning, and the experience can be similar to the use of drugs, in which feelings of pain are replaced by a sense of well-being.

In Cathy's case, there were early traumas: The loss of her sister when she was four and the pain she felt when she first began school. She was a child who was extremely vulnerable to loss and separation.

When children leave home for the first time—to begin college or to enter a prep school—here are some guidelines to remember:

1. Be aware how difficult leaving home can be for some children.

2. Provide continuing emotional support, especially during the first year, even if your attention does not evoke enthusiastic cheers from your child.

3. Make calls and write letters, not excessively but with regularity.

4. Encourage the child to talk about difficult times as well as joyous moments. Cathy's parents, for instance, focused on the good times—they were caught up in their own enthusiasm.

5. Remember that children may feel unwanted and rejected by their parents, even though they consciously chose to leave home and go away to school, as Cathy did.

6. Remember that early experiences of loss can set a pattern for emotional upheavals later in adolescence.

7. Recognize that rejection of sexuality can be a way of expressing a desire not to grow up.

Cathy was critical of her peers and their boy-crazy behavior. She viewed them as childish. Yet it also reflected a childish part of her, the part that wanted to remain a little girl, the part of her most vulnerable to the lure of the cult.

Moving on: The first time

She (*We gave her most of her lives*)
is leaving (*Sacrificed most of our lives*)
home (*We gave her everything that money could buy*)

So it was chronicled in "Sgt. Pepper's Lonely Hearts Club Band," words and music by the Beatles, in celebration of that sad, happy, historic moment of flight, mixed with elation and guilt: leaving home.

The lyric touched many young hearts and distressed older ones when it was written in the late 1960s. It is still an anthem of sorts.

"She . . . is having fun," they sang. "Fun is the one thing money can't buy . . . Something inside that was always denied . . . Bye bye."

As always, young people ponder the decision. If they are not going away to college after high school graduation, can they afford an apartment of their own? To share it, most likely. To have a modest job to pay the rent. To have the freedom to come and go, to enjoy.

"Where did we go wrong," parents may fret, while their offspring lament, "They don't understand . . . that I don't hate them, that I want to be on my own, live my own life."

Moving with Care

It is not easy. For thousands of teenagers, in cities, small towns, and suburban communities, the melody lingers on. But it is difficult to translate rhetoric into reality.

Where does anyone get a decent job at seventeen or eighteen? Where are you, if you are not college-bound or altar-bound? What happens if you lose your job or your car breaks down or you get sick or your roommate moves away?

So many teenagers do remain at home, in their old room— working part-time even if they do attend a local college—scanning the apartment ads, saving up money slowly, waiting.

By living at home, they can afford to keep up an old car or to take a trip somewhere. So many wait before making a big step toward quasi-independence. Many are in school or planning to marry. But what happens to the others—young people who often feel they are neither children nor adults?

Some leave home quickly.

Claire moved into her own apartment when she was just a month past her eighteenth birthday. A week after high school graduation, she landed a job as a secretary in a law firm. Her father did not speak to her for six months. Gina was seventeen when she moved into a suburban house with her college boy friend, dividing food and rent expenses, going to school part-time, working part-time.

Some wait briefly.

Jerry moved out when he was nineteen, a year after graduating from high school. He moved into a four-bedroom house with three other young people, just getting by on what he earned at his warehouse job. His parents did not understand why he and his friends rejected the comforts of home before they were ready to fully support themselves. In their two-story Victorian house, they shared expenses and their girl friends joined them in cooking dinners. Jerry discovered a new sense of family, and after a year his parents reluctantly accepted his decision, though still believing their son should have remained at home until he found a wife to take care of him.

Finally, some young people leave their homes in a state of turmoil.

Late one night, Mike slipped out before his parents could protest. He was only sixteen and a half, and he had no real place to live. Two years later, he found a studio apartment with a friend and, working in a fast-food restaurant, he was just able to afford his share of the rent. Until then, he counted on the hospitality of older friends, who would let him sleep on a living room sofa for a few nights at a time. Often his parents did not know where he was.

Claire's Story

Claire is now in her mid-twenties and her parents have forgiven her. But their relationship is still scarred. Right after graduation, when she and two of her school girl friends found a sunny, one-bedroom apartment, they placed a deposit immediately. Then Claire went home to tell her parents about her decision. She had not wanted to discuss her plans beforehand.

Her parents could not believe that she would move away so quickly and so abruptly. "Do what you think is best," her father said, and walked out of the room. Her mother cried. Two days later, when she moved her belongings into her new apartment, her father said: "I didn't think you were serious." And the following week, when she returned home for dinner—at her mother's invitation—her father refused to sit at the dinner table. He did not speak with her for half a year. "He assumed I was not happy at home. He didn't understand and neither did my mother. But I just wanted my own place."

Claire's parents did find the move difficult to understand. For one thing, it was a move that was not done when they were eighteen. And Claire could not afford even a car, although she didn't need one. She was able to walk to work, and her boy friend had a car of his own. The living arrangements also baffled Claire's parents. For financial reasons, she shared the one-bedroom apartment with two other young women, one sleeping on a studio couch in the living room. At home, she would have had a room of her own, her parents argued. "But this is my own home," Claire insisted.

In their small community, Claire and her friends were still the exception. "Almost no one left home except to get married or to move out of town for a job or school. Perhaps one in ten kids left so soon. When other kids heard about us, we were like heroes for a while."

But moving out can be more horrendous than heroic, she recalled later. Her mother still feels wounded by the move, even though Claire is now in her mid-twenties. And some of her friends had more bruising experiences.

"Some were barred even from coming home for a visit. One was cut out of a will . . . A lot did stay home because of family pressure or lack of money or lack of imagination. I think I made the right decision. But parents can be very hurt, even though none of us meant to hurt anyone."

Gina's Story

Gina was seventeen when she graduated high school. That summer, she moved into a cottage with her boy friend. Her mother, who is a widow with two other children, was deeply upset and hurt, but accepted Gina's decision after a few months.

Gina had landed a clerk's job in a department store and earned enough money to pay for food and utilities. Her boy friend paid the monthly rent and other house expenses, and they came out about even.

She felt lucky. At her parents' home, she had to share a room with her sister. Her new place was much more comfortable, and it became her new home.

"But it can go wrong. I knew that. Like if we split up. Then we'd both probably have to move home. I had another friend, and after she wrecked her car, she had to move home for financial reasons. Another friend had to go back home when her roommate got married. You can't afford an apartment alone, so you have to have a boy friend or another girl to share the costs."

But moving back home?

"My friends told me—it's never the same again."

Jerry's Story

Jerry was able to afford a house of his own by sharing expenses with three friends, including two young women from school.

They each had separate bedrooms, but their life was communal. They shared rent and food costs, divided up household chores, and contributed posters to brighten the living room. Communal life, Jerry found, was less tense than living at home, but he continued to call his parents' place "home" for some years.

Actually, his parents had wanted him to move out. "It had been a hassle for a long time," he remembered. "What they were saying to me was: Go live in the cold cruel world and you'll see how good you had it here. I think they expected me to crawl back home. So I was suddenly on my own."

149

A year after moving into the communal house, his friends decided to have their own Thanksgiving dinner. His roommates and their friends made the entire meal. Jerry's parents were hurt because it was the first Thanksgiving meal he had not spent with them. "You should be with your family," his mother said in a tearful telephone conversation. "But this is my family," he replied, gently.

He did miss his four brothers and sister at first, but not the noise and the congestion. "If you had a girl friend come over, you know, you couldn't go to your own room and lock the door or anything. You had to be in the living room with everyone else. Then if you stayed out late, there were arguments."

At first his family was very angry at him. "They disapproved of anyone moving out so young." he said. "My parents didn't understand why I wanted to be on my own. They'd tell me that at home, I'd have no rent and a full refrigerator and air conditioning. I didn't think they'd ever see my point. But then, when I did move out and had a little more space in my life, I started to get along with them, both my mom and dad, for the first time."

Mike's Story

When Mike first moved away from home, space was a luxury he didn't know. But at nineteen, finally sharing a studio apartment, he felt grown up for the first time. At sixteen he had lived on the couches and floors of friends, working at odd jobs, just getting by.

He finally landed a job in a tire repair shop and made enough money to share the rent with a fellow worker from the shop. There had been much worse times, he recalled, sleeping on the road—in railroad stations or in friends' houses when he was lucky. But the worst years—his teen years—were almost over.

"I learned a lot about responsibility just in the last year—that you got to pay the rent if you want a place of your own. I don't talk to my parents much. We get along okay now. I think they got used to the idea of my being gone. But they didn't like my taking off when I was sixteen. They didn't understand I needed to be free." For many parents, that is the hardest reality.

Parents Facing Realities

For Claire and Gina, for Jerry and Mike, the transition through adolescence was not easy—not for them or for their parents.

Can parents make their lives less painful when confronted with an adolescent who feels he or she must leave home, a child who is ready to move on before his parents can accept the notion?

Yes, they can. Parents can not only make their own lives less painful but, by doing so, they can lighten the burden on their children at this time of crisis. And parents can make their own lives more comfortable by coming to terms with their own feelings about separation, about letting go of their children. It is a process that begins in childhood and has memorable landmarks through the years. Most parents will remember them without difficulty:

- The first day at school.

- The first overnight trip away from home.

- The first extended stay at summer camp or with relatives.

- The first boy friend or girl friend.

- Living away from home at a school or college.

- Moving to a home or apartment of their own.

The central task of parenting is to prepare children for each of these steps, to prepare them to make healthy separations, to function on their own. As the result of the good feelings they have about themselves, they can gain a sense of confidence that they indeed can function in a world of their own making.

Many influences are at play, of course. Teachers, relatives, and peers, as well as the home environment, all shape children's ability to deal with being on their own. Inconsistencies at home can also be a factor. Try to be aware of your own ambivalence about your child's independence. These contradictions can confuse adolescent children.

Often, these inconsistent messages stem from contradictory needs felt by parents themselves—at times deeply rooted and unrecognized by mothers and fathers. Although they want their children to seek real independence, to be confident of running their own future lives, they also want to protect them from the occasional cruelties of ordinary living. The desire is high-minded—but impossible.

Adolescence, which often brings restlessness and the urge to move on, occurs at a time when parents may be approaching crises of their own. Fathers in their early or mid-forties may be confronting unpleasant truths about their early dreams of success or achievement. Midlife crises may be forcing to the surface impossible longings for youth.

Mothers of adolescent children are also likely to face a partial loss of identity at this time, especially if they have staked a sizable share of their emotional lives on child-rearing to the exclusion of other interests and activities outside the home.

Parents who feel unloved by each other or who feel unfulfilled in their personal lives may be even more reluctant to see their children begin to lead independent lives—although they may not be able to admit these feelings to themselves.

Children, of course, will make mistakes. They may be hurt as they learn to stand on their own. But the chances of being hurt would be lessened if they were supported by their mothers and fathers in their earliest maneuvers toward independence, from the time they took their first faltering steps as infants.

Parents can bestow on their children a gift, a message that the world is a safe place rather than a threatening place. If they are overprotective or restrictive, their children will be more likely to feel unsafe and unsure of their capability to function apart from their parents. And as a result, they may perceive the world as being even more unsafe than it is. In this time of upheaval, parents can ease the sense of crisis in the home:

- By listening carefully to their children's reasons for leaving home.

- By trying to separate their own need for their children to remain close to the nest from the needs of their children to move on.

- By acknowledging that they will miss their children and will feel a sense of loss, which is natural.

- By seeking comfort in each other and in friends and in new activities.

- By understanding that their children's move need not be seen as a personal rejection, even when children say that they are leaving home to avoid or escape the control of their parents.

Children may feel they need to leave home to preserve their relationship with their parents. And often, the relationship between parents and children matures and improves in quality after the separation.

So parents need to remain emotionally available to their children after they have moved out. Often, children will speak only of their good feelings about being on their own. But they often experience a mixture of ambivalent feelings—sometimes unfocused and unrecognized—such as loneliness, anxiety, sadness, even rejection.

The relationship between parents and children will change—and it should and must—but it need not end when children find a new place to call home. That is what so many parents worry about: that their children will be gone forever.

This process of reconstruction takes time and energy on the part of both parents and children. And empathizing with the adolescent's point of view often will challenge parents to recall some of their own feelings about leaving home—their ambivalence, their loneliness and sadness, their fears about making it on their own and about growing up.

In some cases, adolescents fear that their parents will be so angry that they will slam the door shut on them—in total rejection—a mirror image of parental fears. For parents, this period can stir up painful memories, but by recalling and confronting them, their recollections from the past can pay off in bridging the gap between themselves and their restless adolescents.

CHILD OF DIVORCE

Gordie: A weekend scene

"Hey, there he is, sitting in front of the house," Jerry said, slowly turning his sedan into the shady street.

Halfway up the block, Gordie, a small eight-year-old in overalls, sat on the edge of the curb, his feet parenthesizing a puddle.

Gordie looked a bit glum. Despite a ripple of a midsummer breeze, the suburban street was dreadfully hot and humid on a Sunday morning in July.

"Are the other kids coming?" Jerry asked his son.

"Just me and Kat," Gordie said.

"Awwww," Jerry groaned. He was disappointed his two other daughters, both teenagers now, would not join him for the regular Sunday outing.

Gordie ran into the house to bring out his sister Kat, who was six. His mother was also in the house, but she would not come out to say hello. Although she and Jerry had been divorced for more than a year, they became either furious or depressed when they saw each other, even for a few minutes.

While Jerry chain-smoked in the car, the two teenage girls came out to say hello. They took turns leaning through the car window to hug their father. First Linda, fifteen, and then Judy, who was fourteen.

"I don't feel too good," said Judy, "and she's gotta go with her girl friends this afternoon," motioning to her sister.

Jerry nodded. It was no big deal. He would see them the next Sunday. But they were beginning to make plans of their own. The handwriting was on the wall.

Then Kat bounded down the front walk and jumped into the front seat, cuddling next to her father. Gordie slid in beside her.

"We went to the beach yesterday," he told his father. "Great waves!"

Jerry smiled.

"Mike took us," Kat chirped, bobbing around on the front seat.

Jerry stopped smiling. Mike was his former wife's fiancé. Even now, he hated the idea that there was someone else in her life.

Judy and Linda leaned against the car door.

"That's a new shirt," Judy said, touching her father's collar.

"You're growing a beard," said Linda, patting her father's face.

"No. I just didn't shave this morning," he said. "By the way, don't forget we're all going to New Hampshire in August.

"Oh, can't we go sooner?" Linda whined.

"Maybe," her father said.

"Yeaaaaaaa," they all cheered.

"See you next Sunday," he called out.

The car pulled away and the two girls watched until the car reached the corner and turned out of sight.

Jerry was taking the two youngest children to the local amusement park, a trip they often made on summer Sundays.

"Did you have a nice Fourth of July?" Jerry asked.

"Oh yeah, we saw fireworks," Gordie said. "But I wish I was with you."

"Me too," Jerry said.

"Mike took us," Kat said.

Jerry said nothing, just drove in silence.

Losing the Kids

Jerry and his wife had been married for seventeen years. Jerry was forty-four now. They had decided to end their marriage a year ago, but it had really been over for a long time. Kat had not been planned. They had just grown apart, grated on each other, fought often, then grew tired of fighting. "But she was beautiful," Jerry said, describing his ex-wife later in the day.

There was also another child, the oldest, a seventeen-year-old boy who had a summer job. Jerry felt very close to him. "He won't go anywhere with that guy Mike," he said, a bit proudly. He paused. "I was the one who wanted the divorce, but I still love her . . . No, I don't. Not really. Oh, God, I don't know."

By noon, both children looked exhausted from the weight of the humidity and the brilliant sunshine. Their $4 ticket to the amusement park entitled them to as many rides as they liked until 3 o'clock, but they were wilting fast.

"We'll go on some more rides and then we'll have some ice cream," Jerry said, trying to keep everyone's spirits up.

Kat wanted her ice cream now. Gordie wanted to play the video games now. Kat wanted to go on the rides, but only if Gordie did. Gordie didn't want to be pulled around by a six-year-old. Besides, he wanted to go on the rides with his father alone. The whining and squabbling went on and on. Finally, Jerry prevailed and the kids went on the rides. Jerry needed a break.

"That was some party last night," said a man who came over to say hello to Jerry. "Yeah," Jerry said. The party had been sponsored by a local chapter of Parents Without Partners. Many of the partygoers—the ex-husbands—had brought their kids to the amusement park that morning.

"Very decadent," the other man joked. During the party, it seems, someone had jumped into the pool without his clothes. Jerry found the party a bore, and he had a hangover. He had met no one he liked. "You see," he said when the man moved on, "you get divorced and you start acting like a kid yourself, going to amusement parks every Sunday and jumping into swimming pools without your clothes."

His own kids, fussing and feuding with each other, were placated by slices of pizza and a couple of glasses of soda. A man in his late twenties and a small boy walked by the pizza stand. The man nodded hello. "I can't believe it." Jerry said. "He was a student of mine when I was teaching high school, and now he's divorced too."

The kids were really cranky by now. Jerry picked up Kat and carried her. She almost dozed off. Gordie wanted to stay in the video arcade, but it was time to go, his father said.

"Sometimes I wonder why I bring the kids here. I think they're as bored as I am. I just can't think of things to do." He took Gordie's hand.

"Stop pulling me around," Gordie whined. Jerry let his son's hand go. "And don't lose me," Gordie said, on a new tack. Jerry felt he could do nothing right.

"Come on." he said. "We'll all have ice cream and then we'll go over to Grandma's for dinner."

At Jerry's mother's house, everyone would feel better. The kids would collapse in silence in front of the TV set, and maybe Jerry would take a nap or read the newspaper. They'd have to wait at least a couple of hours before dinner, and then there was the ride back to their mother's house. At least, he didn't feel that he had to constantly entertain the kids when they were at their grandmother's house. It was a little like being home, at least for the rest of a Sunday afternoon with the kids.

Parenting Part-Time

Sunday in the park with the kids can be an ordeal. And for noncustodial parents in many divorces, it often is. Can parenting part-time be more satisfying than an unamusing park?

It can be, but it takes solid planning and patience. For many divorced and separated couples, of course, joint custody has been a positive response to the problem of child-raising after a breakup.

Geography is an obvious factor. Both parents must remain in their children's school district for a genuine two-home arrangement to work. But even if the children remain with one custodial parent most of the time, joint custody can provide more flexibility and felicity in arranging child-sharing.

The time shared by parent and children tends to be more natural and comfortable and children seem to be happier, even if they must adjust to different styles of living and different rules at each of their homes. Their relationship with each parent tends to be more natural, and they feel less abandoned by the parent who has moved away. If both parents establish new relationships or remarry, their children may have to adjust to a new face in two homes instead of one. But the adjustment problem is probably no more difficult, and it may be easier.

In Gordie's case, his father faced a time crunch in which all his parenting was squeezed into a few hours. The situation was artificial and tension-producing. If possible, parents should try to reach more flexible agreements with regard to child-sharing. Visits should not be limited to a Sunday. Visits during the week, even on an occasional basis, might relieve some of the tension felt by both parents and children.

And because children range in age, the difference in interests and lifestyles should be taken into account when planning visitation schedules. Often, sequential agreements, rather than one fixed plan, can ease the adjustments to the children's needs as they get older, moving through different stages of development. As children mature and reach adolescence, they spend their time differently. Their interests and activities change, and so do their needs. These changes are recognized in good visitation planning.

A four-year old, for instance, could be satisfied with very different arrangements than a ten-year-old would require. At four, a child's most important need is to feel that her mother and father are available, emotionally. So a father might feel comfortable while reading a book or doing a crossword puzzle in the same room with his child. The little boy or girl could be busy playing with blocks or a drawing book but still secure that his parent was there in the room, close by.

At ten, children are more verbal, more able to express and share feelings and experiences. Times spent on a visit with a parent might include some quiet, reflective time, when exchanges of feelings can be made. Communication is more important during this period than filling up the hours with busy activities, barring all time for talk.

In adolescence, there will be times when parents will lose out in competition with their children's friends. Teenagers will have their own interests and friends, and their activities will not always include you. This is a healthy and normal phase of development for a teenager, and it would happen with or without a marital breakup—so try not to take it personally.

The fact of divorce, however, does tend to magnify this normal pattern, heightening the sense of loss of the noncustodial parent. But most likely, these choices in adolescence are not designed to punish the parent.

When Jerry, Gordie's father, learned that his two older daughters had made other plans, it might have helped to recall his own adolescence and how difficult it had been to spend time with his parents—especially when such activities conflicted with more alluring, exciting plans made with friends. This can be true even when parents are very understanding and have a good relationship with their children. It is a part of adolescents' search for their own identity as emerging adults.

If busy teenagers are unavailable on weekends, arrangements for during the week can be a solution. Whether the visits are on weekends or midweek, they should be as natural as possible. Occasionally, full weekend visits might be arranged.

It is reassuring to children of all ages when they have their own bed and belongings in both homes—their own space—even if the luxury of an extra room is not possible. They can still have a real sense of belonging in both homes, rather than being caught in a domestic tug of war.

It is also a treat—and important—to take the children separately on some visiting days. Even an occasional visit is cherished when the child has the parent's exclusive attention, without having to compete with brothers and sisters. These separate visits are special and can deepen the relationship between parent and child even if they happen only a few times a year. Children always remember these extraordinary days, spending time alone with a parent.

Having Fun

Meanwhile, there are years of parenting to carry out on a commuter basis. The familiar amusement park gambit was a bumpy ride for Gordie and his father Jerry, especially when the Sunday visits seemed to become recreation by rote.

Other activities, less complicated and less exhausting on a hot Sunday afternoon, might have given Jerry and his children more of the contact and communication they all needed.

Some shared moments might be very simple:

• Doing homework together can normalize a visit.

• Reading a story out loud might provide some welcome relief from the tedium of the TV.

• Going to a baseball or football game, for instance, offers a chance to share emotions and experiences.

• Playing catch, going bowling, playing Ping Pong are simple activities that can be shared with both young girls and boys.

• Playing board games can bring all the children together.

But more than play can be shared. Often fathers who are diligent about child support payments become resentful even while they are supporting their children's activities. They can feel shut out—in fact, may be shut out—of all the decisions involving the children and everyday events. Often, too, another man has taken their place and sees the children more frequently.

Fathers, when confronted with these feelings, can seek a more active role in the lives of their children. If a boy or girl is taking music lessons or riding lessons or learning how to swim, for instance, a father may arrange to accompany the child on some occasions—to take part in some of these activities and to get some of the credit for caring. He may also take the child shopping for clothes or for equipment and materials needed for special activities—a baseball glove, some sheet music, a saddle—the size, shape, or expense doesn't matter.

But such trips give parent and child a real activity to share, something that might have been done together if there had been no divorce or separation, as if they all were still living at home. In fact, if there had been no breakup, a parent might be less likely to participate in such mundane activities. But after the marital split, everyday events seem more significant, and by taking part, a parent may still be a valued part of the children's lives, remain in the family picture, and in a sense, enjoy a full share in parenting.

Crisis
X

SEXUAL ABUSE

The issue of sexual abuse is a jarring one. Cases of child-molesting, reported at a number of day care centers in late 1984, sent shock waves of anger, fear, and repulsion across the country. If a child cannot find shelter in a day care center, where is a child safe? Many parents have asked each other that question.

Sexual abuse of children is a crisis that has drawn keen public attention in recent years. Perhaps like many social ills, it will crowd center stage for a time and then recede in intensity. It is little comfort, of course, but sexual abuse of children is not a new phenomenon. In fact, most adults probably remember the old warning etched in the memory of childhood: "Don't take candy from a stranger."

How many thousands of pieces of candy remained untaken over the decades! But sexual abuse goes on. Some of the molesters are those strangers with candy in hand or seated with car door open, outside the schoolyard.

In recent years, however, police, teachers, and social scientists have all contributed to a new understanding about sexual molestation, how widespread it is, and, in a great number of cases, how the molesters are not strangers at all. They are often neighbors, baby-sitters, family friends, or relatives. So the shadow of danger is always there.

But parents can protect their children and prepare them to

163

meet the risk of sexual abuse, another sad fact of life for all boys and girls.

When should parents begin?

Early—in early childhood.

And how?

By teaching children to feel good about themselves. It is the first step. A strong sense of self-esteem will make children less vulnerable to sexual abuse and a less likely target for sex offenders. When children are sure that they are loved at home, for instance, they are less likely to be lured by "the promise of love" often made by sexual molesters.

Parents can build this sense of self-respect, a positive way in which children can look at themselves. Here are three suggestions:

- Praise your children often.

- Listen to your children carefully.

- Respect your children's space—both their physical and emotional boundaries.

Praise

Being specific in your praise is an important part of building self-esteem in children. Suppose that a younger brother or sister has been hurt and your child shows concern and is comforting the injured sibling. Rather than saying, "Oh, what a good boy you are," or "What a nice girl you are, to do that," you might say, instead, "You're very special, because you're such a sensitive person when anyone gets hurt."

Or if a child brings home good grades, rather than saying, "Hey, that's terrific about your grades," you might elaborate by adding, "I know how hard you try and it makes me feel so good about you."

Rather than punishing children for mistakes, it is also better to reward positive behavior. For example, if a child has trouble eating dinner without spilling something—milk or a soft drink—it would be better to reward success rather than to criticize failure. At the end of an accident-free meal, an extra dessert or something special to reward good behavior would be more effective than responding to accidents with a scolding or some form of punishment.

And when a child needs to be criticized, it is crucial to focus on the improper act and not on the child himself or herself. For example, if a child lies, rather than calling the child a liar, you might say: "I don't like it when you lie . . . It makes me confused and angry."

If your children have messy rooms and their habits disturb you, rather than say, "You're such slobs," you might make your own feelings known by saying, "I get very uncomfortable when rooms aren't neat, so I'd like you to clean up a little."

Children take in all that their parents say, and it becomes part of their own self-concept—the way they feel about themselves. So when parents must criticize, it is best to criticize the action, not the child.

Part of the strategy of praise is even easier: tell your children you love them. Children need to be told that they are loved. Some children interpret silence as significant, that they are unloved or, even worse, unlovable.

Now, what does this have to do with sexual abuse? A child's first line of defense against the sex offender is self-esteem, which lessens the child's vulnerability to abuse. The child who knows that he or she is loved at home will be less likely to accept the "promises of love" that offenders often offer.

Listening

By listening to children carefully, parents can also lay the foundation of protection for the future. Parents need to take seriously what their children tell them.

Why?

Because children who are sure that their parents will listen also know that their parents will hear and believe them if they have traumatic events to report—even if it is a case of sexual abuse by someone who loves them. It is crucial that parents respond to their children in the same way that they would want to be treated themselves. In these moments of crisis—any crisis, in fact—there are a number of responses that can be avoided:

- Don't become instantly judgmental. Don't say, for example, "Now big boys don't cry."

- Don't become superrational. Don't say, for example, "Oh, you're old enough to know there are no ghosts."

- Don't attempt merely to "cheer up" your child. Don't say, for example, "I know you'll feel better tomorrow."

- Don't deny reality. Don't say, for example, "I'm sure things aren't so bad."

All of these responses tend to shut down children emotionally and do nothing to satisfy their needs to be heard and nurtured.

And in what way does this protect children from sexual abuse? They are the ways in which parents can take their children's words seriously, ways in which they also build self-esteem in their youngsters. It is a preventative step in shaping a child who will be less likely to become a victim.

Children often think they will not be listened to or believed. So if a crisis does come, a child needs to feel that he or she will be heard. Terrifying dreams, for instance, provide a good example of how parents inadvertently cheer rather than listen. Sometimes, they will tell the child, "Oh that was just a nightmare . . . there's nothing to be afraid of," rather than urging the child to talk about the terrors in the dream.

It is comforting to empathize and say, "Oh, I remember how I used to be afraid of monsters in my dreams too, when I was your age." It is another way of showing concern about children's feelings while taking them seriously.

Respecting Space

Respecting the physical and emotional boundaries of children is another way to build self-esteem, and thus to protect your child against sexual abuse.

Adults often hug and kiss children, for instance, whether the child likes it or not. But parents can start early in children's lives to respect their feelings about affection. If children squirm away, feel uncomfortable or complain when adults hug them, it is an opportunity to respect their feelings and their right to be touched or not touched, instead of insisting on showing affection by imposing adult will. Parents also need to be on guard against feeling rejected themselves when a child does draw an emotional line. It is important also to respect a child's privacy—in their bedroom or the bathroom, for instance—in the same way that adults want their privacy respected.

Often children are warned that it is "bad manners" to be assertive. The message is confusing, since a child sometimes behaves in the same way an adult does but is criticized for rudeness, while the adult is praised for being "strong." The need of children to express themselves is not different from an adult's need and should be recognized. If, for example, a child says that he or she does not like some adult—a friend of the family, perhaps—parents might become upset or angry at the child's forthrightness.

But the child is entitled to express an opinion and should not be squelched or told that "children don't talk that way about adults." Such a response makes a dramatic distinction between the rights to which adults and children are each entitled. Such a distinction paints part of the backdrop for child abuse.

Children who are keenly aware of this distinction feel they must do exactly what an adult—any adult—tells them to do. In almost every case, children feel adults loom large as authority figures and are much more important and special than they are. So even when children protest abusive treatment, they can feel controlled by the adults around them, feeling they must obey at all cost.

Remember, too, that adolescent boundaries are often subtle. As children enter adolescence, they may become uncomfortable with the kind of physical and emotional intimacy that they once enjoyed when they were younger. And these changes come at varying ages.

A young girl, for example, may have been called a pet name by her father all through childhood. But in her teens she may not want to be referred to in that childish way any longer. The need should be recognized and respected. A boy who was hugged and kissed by his mother as a child may reject such affection during adolescence. That wish, too, should be respected.

By observing the boundaries of children, parents also encourage their sons and daughters to set and to respect their own boundaries. And in that way they learn that they have a right to be protected, to insist that their boundaries of privacy not be violated by anyone.

Warning Children

In a specific way, parents can prepare their children to deal with dangerous possibilities. These situations can be dealt with in inventive conversations with their children, outlining specific but not nerve-shattering scenes—perhaps in the form of a litany of "What would you do?" questions.

For example:

1. *What would you do if you were walking home from school and someone offered you a ride home?*

   Parents can offer the classic response: "You say no. You say that your mother says you're not supposed to. Then you come home and you tell your mother or father, right away."

2. *What would you do if somebody you knew—the babysitter or a neighbor or a teacher—wanted you to sit on their lap or touch you or play games in a way that made you feel uncomfortable, something you knew you were not supposed to do? Touching—your penis—your vagina—parts of your body where you did not want to be touched?*

   Parents again can tell their children to respond: "No, that's not what I want to do. I have to go home now. My mother says I'm not supposed to do that."

3. *And what would you do if it was someone even closer?*

Parents need not be graphic. They can tell their children that people do bad things and sometimes it might be someone they know well or someone they really love. And if this person wanted to touch them in a way they didn't like, they could still say that they didn't want to do that.

In this way, parents can let their children know that they are aware bad things do happen, and that if they do, the parents will listen and talk about it.

At times, young victims of sexual abuse are not indelibly tainted by the experience. But it is difficult for parents to be comforting and reassuring in such situations, since they are so shaken themselves. An effort can be made to prevent the child from picking up the parents' own sense of trauma.

If they can, parents can encourage their children to talk about the experience. If it is too difficult for the parents, a professional counselor might assist them.

Most important is to allow the child to express how he or she is feeling rather than to tell the child how upset you are feeling—how terrible the situation or event is for you. For a very young child, who has not been physically hurt, the experience will not necessarily be seen as shameful or traumatic unless mothers and fathers reinforce those feelings.

As children get older, they can also be protected by developing good friendships of their own. Often, child abusers use the "special friend" approach, and children who are most vulnerable are lonely, isolated, and unable to make friends. Some children need to be encouraged to take risks and to make special efforts to develop friendships.

Of course, they might be rejected by some playmates, but they can learn to try again—if their parents are standing by to support and encourage them when necessary.

The Most Damaging Abuse

Our society has just begun to face the reality of incest as a widespread social problem. Much remains unknown about its extent and its nature. Several aspects are clear:

- In almost all cases, the relationship between the parents is flawed.

- Often there is a reversal of roles played by daughter and mother.

- Often the father feels inadequate in his relationships with adult women.

- Often both father and daughter crave affection—and the child accepts sexual advances as affection or as the price of affection from the parent.

In cases of father-daughter incest, the most prevalent form, the mother is often compliant. Even if she is aware of the situation, she will remain silent, since she depends on the husband for economic and emotional support. And the daughter's personality mirrors her mother's, becoming more and more compliant and unprotesting as time passes. In some cases, sexual activity is limited to fondling and is never reported to police, teachers, or family. But for Erica, a victim of incest for years, suffering was boundless.

Erica: Victim of incest

The victims almost always endure their ordeal in silence. Like soldiers missing in action, they remain lost for years in a private jungle of fear and guilt. And some of these survivors of traumatized childhood do not emerge into the sunlight until adulthood.

Erica was the daughter of a salesman. She was raised in a middle-income home in Westchester County, in a suburban village just north of New York City. For Erica, the nightmare began at age three. The molester was her father. It began with fondling. Erica remembers the incidents even though other memories of the same period are hazy.

"Then the encounters became more frequent and more forceful. Sexual intercourse began—at least it was partial, with some penetration. By that time, I was seven years old."

She recalled the childhood experiences years later, telling her story for the first time as an adult. Her recollection seemed matter of fact, but the tone was self-protective, as if she was a detached observer. Her voice quavered as she talked, and her eyes glistened. This was, after all, the darkest secret of her girlhood.

"When I was nine, it became full intercourse. It happened on weekends or at night when my mother was asleep. My father often drank, but he was not always drunk. I was hurt so badly in the beginning that I had to stay home from school."

So after six years, Erica's mother found out about the incestuous relationship. But she did not call a doctor or the police. Too ashamed and afraid, she did not want anyone to know. When Erica first told her what her father had been doing, her mother became angry. She blamed Erica—for allowing her father to take advantage, perhaps for encouraging it. And she acted as if nothing really happened.

The attacks continued, but by the time Erica was eleven, her mother became apprehensive. What if Erica became pregnant? For the first time, she called the police. That afternoon, two detectives came to Erica's house and wrote down her story. But Erica was afraid. So she said exactly what her mother told her to say:

"I remember that my mother told me what to tell the police, that it had just happened one time, only once. I signed a lot of papers and my mother stood over me the whole time so there was no chance I'd change the story or say something else. There was no chance they'd find out the truth and the police didn't question the story my mother invented."

Later, one of the detectives, in fact, told Erica's mother that her daughter probably was partially responsible for the incident. Erica's father was charged in court, but he was permitted to plead guilty to an assault charge and his jail sentence was suspended. Placed on probation, he came home that afternoon. The next incestuous assault took place that weekend.

After the courtroom appearance, he felt he would never be accused again. The attacks became frequent—sometimes daily, sometimes more than once a day. The nightmare went on for six more years, until Erica was seventeen and had finished high school.

So Many Years

Erica has only a vague grasp of her feelings during this period.

"I remember being scared all the time. I was too afraid to tell my teachers or my friends. Certainly I would not go to the police. I felt I was the one who was doing something wrong—that there was something about me that made him do it. I always wanted to be different. Maybe if I was fatter or thinner—anything—he would stop."

She could not talk to her mother, and the burden was devastating. She knew that if she spoke out, it would have caused a domestic disaster.

"We would have no one to support us. It would have been instant poverty. That was what my mother was most afraid of. That my father would be thrown in prison. And then how could she support my younger sister and brother and me? How could she care for three children? Once, when I complained again, she said to me: 'Someday you'll be old enough and leave home and then what will I do?' It was crazy but that's what she said."

Years later, as an adult talking with other incest victims, Erica learned that the fear of abandonment and poverty in the family were part of a pattern shared by many incest victims as well as victims of spouse abuse.

Why did Erica submit? She had asked herself the question many times.

"You submit because of force. But there are other pressures playing on you as a child. You're afraid you will be denied love. Or that you won't be fed. Or you'll be thrown out of the house. Sometimes, men like my father can be nurturing at other times. My father was. But he was very erratic. At times, he'd threaten to hurt my little sister or brother. And he warned me that if he went to jail, no one would take care of us. He also told me that my mother didn't believe me and hated me for making up lies."

So during her high school years, Erica went through a change of attitude. She suddenly realized how alone she was. There was no one to protect her. "It was like being in a concentration camp. Maybe I believed in justice when I was younger. Someone would come along and rescue me, some teacher or policeman or relative. But by the time I got into high school, I knew that wasn't true. I was alone."

The nightmare was endless. Her father's power permeated the house. Erica recalls: "I would walk into my room and suddenly there was a hand, reaching out from behind the door, covering my mouth. Or I would be in bed, asleep, and the hand would reach down, grabbing me. Even the bathroom was not safe. My father was everywhere."

From time to time, Erica did complain to her mother, who became furious. "First she'd tell me that I ought to have come to her sooner. Then she'd slap me and say I was lying. Once she told my father about my complaining and he beat me. I learned to remain silent, and after a while my mother didn't seem to really care what was happening."

In school, the secret was closely guarded. Erica pretended to be "normal." Running away was out of the question. Once, when her younger sister took off, she was caught and her father beat her severely. "So I decided to wait, to leave when it was safe, when I couldn't be forced to come back. I was so afraid of being beaten, I was too afraid to try, even when I was sixteen years old."

Around her, the joy and fun of her classmates seemed puzzling. When they laughed or joked, Erica didn't know how they felt. They seemed to speak a different language. Her own childhood, she recalls, had ended before she was seven years old.

Keeping the Secret

"I could never be a child. Never be happy. It takes such energy to keep the secret. I tried so hard to act like other kids, but I was always afraid the secret would slip out."

Erica had no boy friends and didn't want any. But then, her father would not have allowed her to go out on dates. She had to account for every minute of her time. Her father did not want to take any chances on the family secret.

A lifetime of assaults ended when Erica graduated from high school and moved out of the house, sharing an apartment with a girl friend, getting a job as a clerk, just making ends meet. But her fears lasted for years. Even when friends were in the apartment, her father would be there in spirit, lurking in back of a door, behind a chair. "At any moment, a hand might reach out and grab me. So I felt."

Erica went into therapy in her early twenties after a brief marriage ended. It was a typical match for an incest victim—a verbally abusive spouse, insensitive to her childhood traumas. Once, when she had summoned up the courage to tell him about her father, he shrugged and warned her, "Just don't do it again."

For Erica, his reaction reaffirmed her notion about the world, that she could trust no one—not her mother, her husband, the police, no one.

When her marriage ended, a friend recommended a therapist, and Erica began to examine her past. Later, after more than six years of separation, she saw her father one more time and confronted him with the truth. Why did he do it? That was all she wanted to know.

"He denied it ever happened," Erica said. And she has not seen her parents again. "They both refuse to admit that anything ever happened. They can't face it. So I've stopped asking. But I don't feel angry now. No revulsion or hatred. I don't feel anything."

For Erica, the memory has lingered. For years, she lived in silence. In school, there were no teachers who even mentioned the problem of incest. "So you grow up and time passes, but you still feel you ought to be punished, like it was all your fault."

GROWING UP

A seminar in living

The lives of young people are shaped in part by forces beyond their homes and schools, by attitudes and ideas that were formed generations ago.

Some years ago, a remarkable high school teacher named Yves LeMay created a special seminar to reflect the changing times. Designed for older teenagers, it was LeMay's favorite project at the time of her death in an airplane crash during a Christmas holiday.

Just before the vacation, LeMay invited members of her seminar to her home for an afternoon of summing up: to recount for themselves and each other some of the things they had learned about themselves and the world around them—and how they had changed—during the school year.

The teenagers, all sixteen or seventeen, spoke with candor. Perhaps they might have been more hesitant if their parents had been there. They all felt they had been on a special trip with their teacher.

It was a trip not usually taken by teenagers—a guided tour through inner space, where the consciousness of sex roles is secretly shaped. For these young travelers—about a dozen of them—there had been a kind of blinking amazement at their discovery: themselves, as young women.

"What did I discover?" one of them mused. "That I liked myself, first of all and my chest too," she added with a giggle,

Another said: "I was brought up to think that I was going to be a housewife, and that was that. I know now that I've got other choices."

And her classmate added: "All of a sudden we're realizing that there's nothing wrong when females want sex just as much as guys."

They sat in a circle on the floor, stretched across the rug, or draped themselves over the living room furniture, rapping about being young women in a new age. Their discoveries, they said, had been pleasing, but saddening and infuriating as well.

"We've got our own identity . . . We're not just somebody's girl friend," one of them said. "I just realized—my father is the only one who sits in an armchair at the dinner table," another said.

Their work through the year had been very personal: an amalgam of sociological, psychological, and common sensical observations. They talked about TV and magazine ads, women in history, the scarcity of real heroines in literature, how women picked their careers, how marriage contracts got that way.

"We talk about everything," LeMay explained to a visitor: about the way little girls seem to stand passively with their hands behind their back in the illustrations in children's books, about the way females are taught to think about their bodies, about the way we live.

LeMay asked her students: What were some of the ideas that you felt were revolutionary? Responses varied:

"Looking at marriage contracts in a new way," one said.

"Birth control," said another.

"Getting to like ourselves."

"Being able to verbalize what we're thinking."

"Becoming aware of a lot of stuff . . . like how much we rely on the opposite sex to make our lives worthwhile, without thinking about it."

"Discovering that what we do ourselves is the most important thing."

Many of the ideas were new, they said.

"So who am I to you?" LeMay asked.

"A teacher," someone said.

"A friend," said another.

"But," LeMay interjected, "not an authority . . . I'm an authority only on my own feelings."

Myself, My Dream

In some of their seminars they had talked about them-selves—what they liked about themselves and what they did not. For many adolescents, talking about their bodies is diffi-cult. The difficulty was something they shared.

"I just feel that people ought to realize their bodies are wonderful things. They ought to get to know their own before they try to get to know somebody else's," one of the young women said.

Then there were the taboos. "Things that are so frowned on," another student said. "Like touching yourself. You'd never tell anyone. How many young women are really aware of what the inside of their bodies are like? Dark and mysterious. But it's you, it's your body!" She hesitated. "Last year, I never would have been able to say something like that," the young woman added.

The dialogue continued.

Sue said: "I was always against cheerleading and people used to put me down for that. Then I went out for track and I was a manager of the football team last year. And people would say that all I wanted was to be around the boys. That's all they could think of."

Helen told the group: "Last year, my boy friend was presi-dent of the student council. I used to spend all my time waiting for him. So I finally got a job after school and the job pushed us even more apart. But I had started feeling like I was just his girl friend, instead of feeling like I was myself. Well, I want to feel like myself, not like I'm just some part of someone else."

Marti recalled: "You sit home and wait for a call. You tell a girl friend that you'll see her that night. But it really means that you'll see her if your boy friend doesn't call. But how many times does a guy cancel his plans that way? Well, we're learning now that if we choose to, we don't have to play that role."

Donny's view drew many nods of recognition: "I never expected to be a housewife anyway, but I've learned that males are also expected to do a lot of things that are tough to do. They're under a lot of pressure too. So people look at this group and they think that things are changing only for females. But everything's changing."

Another senior recalled that she had wanted to play the bassoon in a symphony orchestra some day. But she recalled that when she was in junior high school, "boys told you that you were trying to act like a guy." But that wasn't true. "I just wanted to be myself."

Being yourself was often sexual. Everyone agreed with that. And sexual desires and attitudes were both personal and varied. They all agreed on that.

"I never limit myself to one boy . . . I'm too young for that. I want experience," one of the more candid seniors spoke out. "If I meet someone I'm attracted to, I know I might have sex and I don't think to myself that this is the last boy in my life. Girls have started to think that they have a right to pleasure too."

So the old double standard raised its head. One of the juniors recalled that she had recently visited her sister's college campus. One of the older guys, she said, had called her a "good-looking chick," and she was furious at the phrase. "My sister warned me that when I got to college I'd better hide my feelings a little more. Well, it really upset me because I felt it was such a demeaning word, even if the guy didn't mean it that way."

It's the double standard, one of her friends said. "Why is it that a guy is looked up to if he sleeps around, and we're put down for it?"

It's absurd, observed the experienced senior. "Some guy puts the move on a girl and he thinks he's a big-time operator—like he's really putting something over on her—and all along, she's just as interested as he is."

So the subject of talking about sex with boys came up. "It's fantastic if you can talk to your boy friend about it. I mean, I think if we can, we've accomplished a great deal," one of the students said.

"Once I told a boy friend that I felt like kissing him and he said he was supposed to make the first move. Then some boys will go around and tell all their friends what you said."

During the year, all of them had exchanged stories about sexuality on the job—summer jobs, part-time jobs, and the like. "Once, I asked my boss how long my job would last and he said it depended on how good I was and I said I was very competent and he said he didn't mean at my job."

"We can't seem to have any relationship without sex becoming a big issue," a senior interjected. "Now I'm not a virgin and I admit it. I think sex is great. But it bugs me when my sexuality is used by people to get something for themselves. That's ugly."

LeMay pointed out: "In such a class, we don't talk only about sex. We focus on books, movies, language, on the hidden persuaders of sexism." When the seminar was ending, one of the young women was talking about friendships with other girls in her school. No, she said, she still preferred the company of boys. But she had learned to share her feelings for the first time, and she was learning more about herself and about other young women. "It's good to know I'm not alone," she said.

A Seminar for the Home

At home, parents too can help teenagers—girls and boys—to adjust to a society that is growing more conscious about sexist behavior and attitudes, even when it is unconscious. And both young men and women about to enter college or the workaday world can be strengthened by such guidance.

The subject of "what a boy really is" and "what a girl really is" are topics that were never part of traditional child-rearing. But parents can aid their offspring to deal with the feelings of crisis when they are confronted with conflicts between traditional notions of "how you should act" and the way they perceive things really are.

By seeking to encourage flexibility in the sex roles played out by their sons and daughters, parents can encourage their children to be more independent. For example, a teenage boy who can iron his own shirts and cook his own meals, or a teenage girl who can change the spark plugs in her car or fix an electric wire on a toaster, will feel more self-sufficient and less dependent on the opposite sex, both during adolescence and in later years.

Parents can also urge their children to develop skills and traits that were traditionally associated with one gender or the other. A young woman, who is sensitive and admires her own domestic skills, could also feel free to explore her strong drive to achieve in the professional world. And a young man, who is geared toward success and upward mobility in the business world, could also feel free to explore his urges to be nurturing and tender with children.

How do parents shape their children's sex roles?

Children certainly learn by watching, so parents become powerful role models for their children at an early age, long before some parents might suspect that future attitudes were being molded. If fathers, for instance, refuse to wash or dry the evening dishes or if mothers insist that it's "my kitchen," then their behavior is likely to be reflected in the way their children act in their own homes when they grow up.

Many parents, of course, have retained and revere traditional sex roles in their home. But they still may want to prepare their children to be more flexible and open to a wider range of options in the future. So it is helpful for parents to carefully monitor their own behavior with each other as well as with their children.

At times, you might try the opposite of what comes naturally by asking your son for example, to join in the household chores or your daughter to take out the garbage—that one last bastion of male domination.

But much earlier, parents can introduce sex role flexibility, as early as the purchase of the child's first toys. And they might refrain from telling their children that "boys don't play with dolls" or that "little girls shouldn't climb trees." In fact, the "unisex look" in the playground is already a reality, in both the real-life community and the world of TV, with little boys and girls both wearing jeans or comfortable play clothes. Older generations remember how grade-school-age girls were hampered by their unwieldy patent-leather shoes and their dresses, which were to remain spotless.

Will these revised views of sex roles turn your son into a sissy or transform your daughter into a little tough guy? The message children will hear is much less complicated or worrisome. And when they are encouraged to develop so-called masculine and feminine social traits, they are more likely to feel, simply enough, that they are first of all a person.

SUMMING UP

While we have related the stories of children in crisis, we
also have written about parenting—perhaps the most difficult
task of all, the one for which we are the least prepared.

Ideal parenting requires that we provide for our children
an atmosphere in which their potential can flourish. A happy
childhood, a tension-free home, understanding parents, and a
feeling of security are all needed to lead children gently
through their most vulnerable and impressionable years.

How do we learn to give these gifts to our children?

It is unlikely that most of us have experienced the kind of
childhood we wish for our own child. Our memories of childhood are often an illusion. We don't really remember our very
early and most important years.

While some memories may linger, they are often vague. Often, with luck, we can remember how we felt on a few occasions, but it is more likely that we will recall the event and not the feeling surrounding it. Some of us have distorted memories of our early lives and we have forgotten much of the anger and frustration and pain we endured as children. So we have forgotten the little child within us who is angry and hurt. We need to feel compassion for this part of ourselves.

Intellectual knowledge is not enough. Looking back, we see that when we were angry as children, it was because we were suffering unbearable pain or humiliation and often were not allowed to express it. It is not the pain that caused trouble, however, but the fact that it was never allowed free expression.

What we all needed was a dependable person in our early childhood to whom we could express angry and painful feelings without the fear that that person would leave us—someone who would take us seriously and respect how we felt. Without this support, we would be apt to forget those feelings.

As parents who have forgotten these childhood pains, we may find it more difficult to stay attuned to our children when they are angry or in pain. But if we listen carefully, our children can remind us how we once felt, years ago. And as we recall our past, we will be more able to empathize with our children and to encourage them to tell us how they feel.

If children can express their feelings, they will be less likely to suffer in self-destructive ways. They can endure the most traumatic experiences if we as parents are there to support them.

We may find many reasons to avoid recognizing the deep pain and rage of our children. We want to protect them from suffering. But children are actually deprived when this "protection" is offered, because they learn to cope with painful feelings as they experience them and see that they can survive. Children need us to be with them through their suffering, and they grow stronger with such support.

Parents too can grow in strength by keeping open channels of communication within the family. Here are some recommendations:

1. Express what you like about your spouse as a parent.

2. Ask your children on occasion: "How are we doing?" In earlier generations, children never felt they had a right to answer that question. Nor did parents pose it.

3. You might try to make a positive statement each day about at least one member of the family—adults and children.

4. You might try to spend some time alone with each of the children—special time—that is keenly remembered, even if it cannot happen often.

Our Children

The young people in these pages have become a special family for us. We were saddened by their pain and heartened by their courage.

In looking back on these troubled families, we find an urgent message in almost all their stories: The art of parenting is best served when parents are aware of their own early experiences.

So it is best to avoid ridiculing children, even when their passing infatuations are carried to outrageous proportions—honoring the punk star or movie legend of the day, the most odd or seemingly inappropriate heroes, who amuse, puzzle, or annoy adults.

During these times, parents may remember their own youthful flights of fantasy. They come at a time of great emotional uncertainty, when teenagers may feel a need to identify with the strengths and virtues of passing heroes or fleeting social movements. These feelings can be carried to extremes, of course, but in dealing with all children and adolescents, patience and kindness can often defuse emotional time bombs in the earliest stages.

Try to recall the fragile defenses of childhood. Even "tough" children, who act-out dramatically, may really feel so incompetent, so unsure of themselves, that a mere look or remark from a parent is all that is needed to confirm their worst fear—that they are worthless.

Ripples of Trouble

Throughout childhood and adolescence, trouble is predictable, a natural part of life. So it is useful for parents to reexamine their family environment continually, on guard for the ways their offspring tell them that something is wrong.

The problem may be rooted in an old wound—an early trauma of separation and abandonment—an event that could not be avoided or went unnoticed, as in the case of Randy, who felt so alone that he wanted to die.

But a wave of suicidal feeling is just one of many warning signs. Parents are familiar with a full spectrum of acting-out behavior—with alcohol, drugs, and sex, by running away from home, cutting classes, misconduct at home or in school, getting hurt. And there are more ambiguous signals: loss of appetite, forgetfulness, insomnia, extreme fearfulness, fatigue, changes in academic success.

Be prepared to listen and respond. Often, the crises of childhood may be set off by events that are far less dramatic than a death in the family. There may be deep feelings stirred up after the loss of a childhood friend, the end of an adolescent romance, even the absence of a parent away on a trip. Or events may be perceived as too "ordinary" to cause alarm—such as the birth of a child, when parents may seem more distant to their other children.

About Therapy

In these pages we have suggested ways in which parents can intervene when they become aware of crises in the lives of their children. But at times they will not be able to handle a crisis alone. Professional counseling is available—and seeking it is not a sign of failure. Often, by the time a counselor or therapist enters the scene, problems have become too complicated for parents to deal with.

Seeking professional advice, in fact, can open new doors of understanding between children and their parents. It can be a beginning, a parental approach that says: Let us face the problem.

APPENDIX:
SEEKING HELP

When children are in crisis, parents are frequently faced with a crucial decision: Should they seek help outside the home?

To many parents, the phrase "professional help" seems foreboding, implying that they have failed as parents.

Seeking professional help also can mean a great commitment of energy, time and, at times, a considerable amount of money as well. They must also overcome the persistent notion that "only crazy people" need and seek psychological help from professionals.

So here are some suggestions to help parents in choosing the best strategy for their child and their family. Often, the first question asked is: "Who can I talk to?" There are a number of people who can be approached. For example:

1. *The teacher.* Since teachers spend hours with their students, they often can help mothers and fathers to make a decision. Teachers may have an insight into the child's ability to relate to his or her studies and to classmates. And teachers can often identify a child who needs professional help.

2. *The school psychologist.* A psychologist working within the school system is in a unique position to work with reading experts, guidance counselors, teachers, and others in the

educational community. Often, a school psychologist can suggest how parents and the school can work together to help a troubled child.

3. *The psychologist in the community*. Children may have difficulty in school and at home for many reasons, either connected with emotional or motivational problems or perhaps with learning disabilities. When a child is carrying an emotional burden that is too heavy, teachers and school psychologists may suggest a mental health expert in the community.

4. *Resource people*. In seeking professional help, parents may want to consult with people in the community before deciding on the form of therapy most suitable for their child. A number of people can make recommendations, including:

   a. The family pediatrician.

   b. Experienced teachers and school counselors.

   c. Other parents who have sought help for their child and themselves—and who feel good about the results.

5. *The choices*. Most parents who seek help will turn to a professional in one of several fields:

   a. A clinical psychologist—a mental health practitioner who has either a master's degree or a doctorate. Requirements vary, but in addition to educational experience, supervised work with patients for a number of years is usually a prerequisite for a clinical psychologist.

   b. A psychiatrist—a medical doctor who has completed a hospital residency in psychiatry. A psychiatrist is permitted to prescribe medication to a patient. Their approaches to problems vary greatly, from crisis intervention to in-depth therapy.

   c. A psychoanalyst—a trained mental health practitioner who has usually completed graduate work in psychology, psychiatry, or social work. The analyst is required to master psychoanalytic therapy and has had clinical experience under senior analysts. In addition, he or she must undergo personal analysis, to free the therapist from personality biases and from emotional conflicts that might interfere with the ability to understand and help others.

d. A social worker—a therapist who holds a master's degree and usually has had at least two years of supervised clinical experience.

e. A counselor—a practitioner who may have less extensive professional training but is skilled in helping children and adolescents during times of crisis. Included in this category are family counselors, paraprofessionals, and mental health workers, often working on the staff of community clinics and hospitals.

6. *Checking on credentials.* Parents can and should be direct in asking professionals in the mental health field about their training, their experience, and their approach to therapy. Information about professionals may also be obtained through such agencies as the American Psychiatric Association, the American Psychological Association, and the National Association of Social Workers.

Community and religious leaders also may be able to comment on the choice of a professional, based on their own experiences in helping other parents. In many communities, crisis hot lines will also refer callers to mental health agencies. In some cities and counties, adolescent and children's centers have been established to aid children in crisis. And in many counties, local mental health associations will refer parents to counseling agencies and to professionals.

In addition, information may be obtained from local social welfare agencies, from local hospitals, or from the psychology department of a university in the area. A number of national associations also will provide information if local sources are not available. Some of these agencies include:

National Medical Association, Chicago, Illinois.

National Association of Social Workers, Washington, D.C.

Family Service Association of America, New York, New York.

American Psychological Association, Washington, D.C.

National Mental Health Association, Alexandria, Virginia.

American Psychiatric Association, Washington, D.C.

National Association for the Advancement of Psychoanalysis, New York, New York.

Credentials, however, do not guarantee a good therapist. Recent research has shown that the outcome of psychotherapy is greatly influenced by the compatibility of the patient and the therapist. It is crucial that the child feel genuinely cared for by the therapist. Parental involvement in the process is often helpful. As our case histories demonstrate, it is often the relationship between child and parent that is a source of the trouble.

As a parent gains insight into his or her own contribution to this painful relationship, changes can take place. And when parents change their expectations, their behavior can also change, which will prompt changes in their child's responses.

In the process of introducing their children to therapy, parents can make therapy or counseling less threatening. For instance, they can describe the therapist, counselor, or psychologist as a person who talks with many children. Children might be reassured to know that their sessions will be very private and that the therapist has helped other boys and girls. Most of all, children should understand that they are not being punished. Later, parents may find it difficult to avoid asking questions, but it is best to respect the child's wish to privacy concerning the meetings with the therapist.

INDEX

ABOUT THE AUTHORS

Patricia Doyle is a psychotherapist who has specialized in the treatment of children and parents for more than a dozen years.

As the parent of three grown children, she writes from both her professional and personal experience. She lectures, conducts workshops and serves as a consultant in schools in New York City and on Long Island.

She has been a member of the psychology faculty and has taught developmental and adolescent psychology at St. Joseph's College and the City University of New York. She is also a Member in Training at the National Psychological Association for Psychoanalysis.

David Behrens is a staff writer with *Newsday*. Specializing in issues of social change, he has written often about youth and family problems, the women's movement, male-female relationships, and drug-related problems.

In 1972 Behrens was part of a seven-member team which won a Pulitzer Prize for "The Heroin Trail," a series on the impact of drug traffic. He also won a National Headliners Award in 1971 for a profile of the death of a civil rights activist who became a drug user.

In 1982 Behrens was named in *Ms.* magazine's tenth anniversary issue as one of the magazine's forty Heroes of the Decade for coverage of the women's movement since the 1970s. He has also written for the *Newsday Sunday Magazine, Maclean's, In These Times, Ms., Glamour* and *Family Circle*. In 1985, Behrens won a Page One Award given by the New York Newspaper Guild for a two-part series on poverty in a South Carolina town.

Catalog

If you are interested in a list of fine Paperback
books, covering a wide range of subjects
and interests, send your name and address,
requesting your free catalog, to:

McGraw-Hill Paperbacks
11 West 19th Street
New York, N.Y. 10011